# NETHERLANDS
## in Pictures

Francesca Davis DiPiazza

Twenty-First Century Books

# Contents

Lerner Publishing Group, Inc., realizes that current information and statistics quickly become out of date. To extend the usefulness of the Visual Geography Series, we developed www.vgsbooks.com, a website offering links to up-to-date information, as well as in-depth material, on a wide variety of subjects. All the websites listed on www.vgsbooks.com have been carefully selected by researchers at Lerner Publishing Group, Inc. However, Lerner Publishing Group, Inc., is not responsible for the accuracy or suitability of the material on any website other than www.lernerbooks.com. It is recommended that students using the Internet be supervised by a parent or teacher. Links on www.vgsbooks.com will be regularly reviewed and updated as needed.

Website address: www.lernerbooks.com

Twenty-First Century Books
A division of Lerner Publishing Group, Inc.
241 First Avenue North
Minneapolis, MN 55401 U.S.A.

web enhanced @ www.vgsbooks.com

Library of Congress Cataloging-in-Publication Data

DiPiazza, Francesca, 1961–
　Netherlands in pictures / by Francesca Davis DiPiazza.
　　p.　cm. — (Visual geography series. Second series)
　Includes bibliographical references and index.
　ISBN 978-0-7613-4628-9 (lib. bdg. : alk. paper)
　1. Netherlands—Juvenile literature. I. Title.
DJ18.D57 2011
949.2—dc22　　　　　　　　　　2009043332

Manufactured in the United States of America
1 – BP – 7/15/10

# INTRODUCTION

The Kingdom of the Netherlands is a small country on the northwestern coast of Europe. Home to 16.5 million people, it is the most densely populated nation in Europe. The people who live there are called Dutch. People sometimes call the country Holland. North Holland and South Holland are just two of the country's twelve provinces, or counties. Historically, they were the richest regions and the center of Dutch trade. The capital city, Amsterdam, is in North Holland.

The Netherlands borders the North Sea—an arm of the Atlantic Ocean. Much of the country's land lies at or below sea level. Hundreds of years ago, the Dutch began to build windmills to harness wind power. The windmills pumped water out of swampy or underwater pieces of land. Seawalls called dikes protect the reclaimed land, where people have built farms, cities, and ports.

In earlier centuries, the Netherlands was made up of independent regions with separate rulers. In the 1500s, Dutch ambitions and a good location on trading routes made the Netherlands a major player in

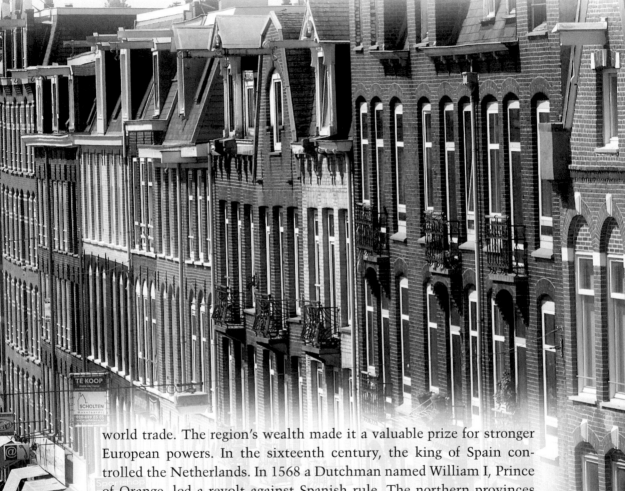

world trade. The region's wealth made it a valuable prize for stronger European powers. In the sixteenth century, the king of Spain controlled the Netherlands. In 1568 a Dutchman named William I, Prince of Orange, led a revolt against Spanish rule. The northern provinces unified against Spain. In 1581 they declared their independence and formed the United Provinces of the Netherlands. This was the beginning of the modern Netherlands.

During the 1600s, Dutch trade grew and brought even more wealth to the Netherlands. With more than sixteen thousand ships, the country was a leading seafaring power. The Dutch were almost always at war. They established settlements and colonies around the world, including North America. The Netherlands also opened its doors to people fleeing persecution in other lands. Dutch culture flourished in this era, called the Golden Age. Rich merchants bought art and thus supported many outstanding artists, including the world-famous painter Rembrandt.

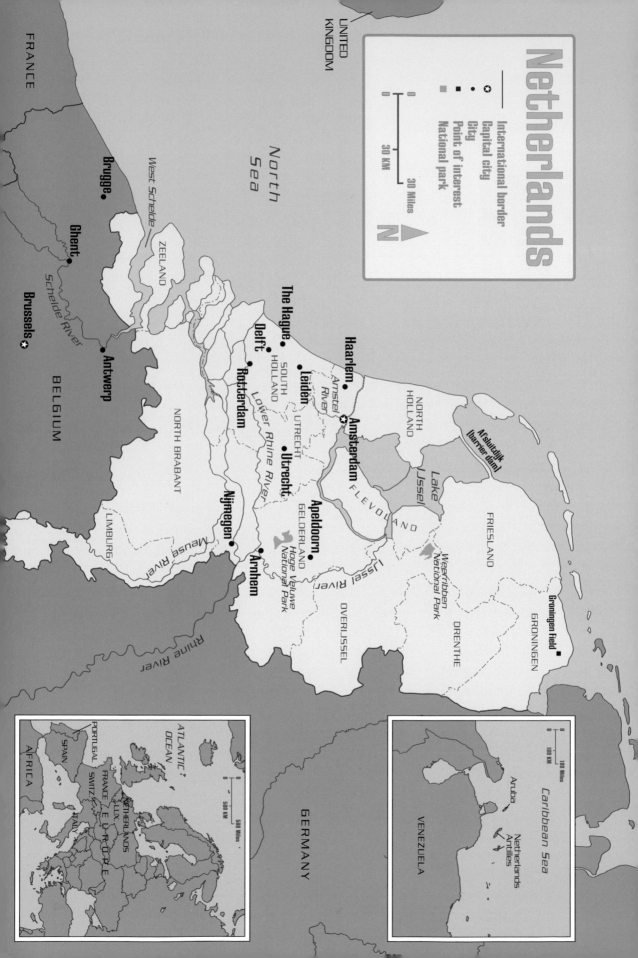

# Netherlands

International border
Capital city
City
Point of interest
National park

0        30 KM
0        30 Miles

N

UNITED KINGDOM

FRANCE

North Sea

Brugge

Ghent

Brussels

Antwerp

BELGIUM

West Schelde

Scheldt River

ZEELAND

The Hague

Delft

Leiden

Rotterdam

SOUTH HOLLAND

Haarlem

Amstel River

Amsterdam

NORTH HOLLAND

UTRECHT

Utrecht

Lower Rhine River

NORTH BRABANT

LIMBURG

Meuse River

Nijmegen

Arnhem

Apeldoorn

GELDERLAND

Hoge Veluwe National Park

IJssel River

FLEVOLAND

Lake IJssel

Afsluitdijk (barrier dam)

FRIESLAND

Weerribben National Park

OVERIJSSEL

DRENTHE

Groningen Field

GRONINGEN

Rhine River

GERMANY

ATLANTIC OCEAN

PORTUGAL

SPAIN

AFRICA

FRANCE

LUX.

SWITZ.

ITALY

NETHERLANDS

EUROPE

0        500 KM
0        500 Miles

Caribbean Sea

Aruba

Netherlands Antilles

VENEZUELA

0        100 KM
0        100 Miles

The Kingdom of the Netherlands formed in 1815. In 1848 the kingdom adopted a new constitution. It set up an elected parliament (legislature) and made the king's role mostly symbolic. The Dutch believed that people should control their own lives and that government should serve the people. The Dutch also valued religion and philosophy, and many Dutch writers and thinkers debated how best to lead a worthy life.

In the late 1800s, the nation's industries grew and many people moved to cities for work. Helped by politically active churches, these urban workers gradually won many social benefits from the government. The improvements included free education and health care.

In the twentieth century, Germany occupied the Netherlands during World War II (1939–1945). After the German defeat, the Dutch rebuilt cities and industries that war had destroyed. The new United Nations, a global peacekeeping organization, set up many of its offices in the Dutch city The Hague. The colonial era gradually ended, and many people from former Dutch colonies moved to the Netherlands.

In 1993 the Netherlands was one of the founders of the European Union (EU). The EU removed all barriers to trade among member nations. These changes helped the Netherlands's economy grow.

The modern Netherlands is a mix of old and new. The Dutch still use wind power, though high-tech turbines have replaced most windmills. Tulips, first popular during the Golden Age, blanket fields in spring. Protecting the nation's land from the sea remains a constant and costly battle. Land is scarce, and the nation's people—who come from many places—face the challenge of living in close quarters with one another. The Netherlands remains a dynamic world business leader. Despite an international financial crisis that began in 2008, the Dutch economy is stable and healthy. Centuries of battling against the sea have shaped the Dutch into a hardworking, efficient, and inventive people. They look to the future with hope.

 Visit www.vgsbooks.com for links to websites with up-to-the-minute information about the Netherlands as well as downloadable maps and photographs of the Netherlands.

# THE LAND

The Netherlands is a small, flat country in the coastal lowlands of north-western Europe. The North Sea (part of the Atlantic Ocean) borders the nation on the west and north. Germany sits east of the Netherlands. Belgium lies to the south. The island of Great Britain, part of the United Kingdom, lies 90 miles (145 kilometers) to the west, across the North Sea. The Netherlands covers 16,036 square miles (41,532 sq. km). It is about half the size of the state of Maine. The nation is part of the Kingdom of the Netherlands. This kingdom also includes two small, self-governing Caribbean islands: the Netherlands Antilles and Aruba.

 ## Topography

The word *Netherlands* means "lowlands," and 27 percent of the country lies below sea level. Early settlers built earthen walls, called dikes, to hold back the North Sea. With these barriers in place, the Dutch pumped the seawater from the land. They built towns and set up farms on the reclaimed land.

The Netherlands is mostly flatland, with few hills. Geographers, however, divide the country into two parts. The High Netherlands region covers five inland provinces. The Low Netherlands includes the coastal provinces of South Holland and North Holland.

### HIGH NETHERLANDS

The High Netherlands occupies the eastern and southeastern parts of the country. Sandy plains and low hills mark the landscape. Within this region is the nation's highest point, Vaalser Mountain (1,053 feet, or 321 meters, above sea level). In the delta of the south central Netherlands is a zone of islands and peninsulas (fingers of land). A delta is an area of sediment at the mouth of a river.

The sandy soil of the High Netherlands supports most of the country's pine forests. Farmers must use fertilizers to help crops grow in the poor soil. In some parts of the region, the Dutch government has created nature preserves and recreational areas.

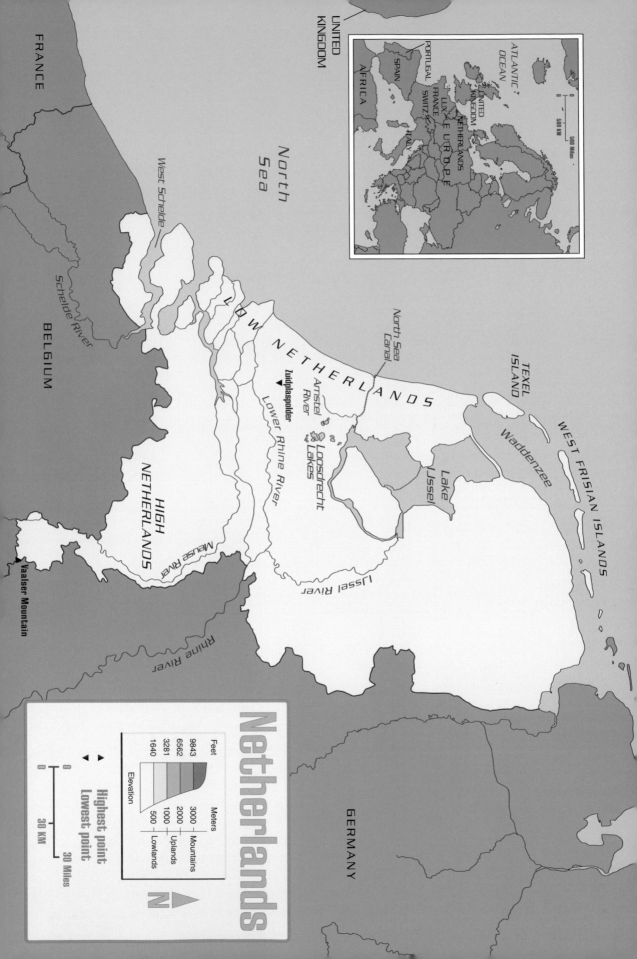

FRANCE

UNITED KINGDOM

North Sea

West Schelde

Schelde River

BELGIUM

LOW NETHERLANDS

North Sea Canal

Zuidplaspolder

Amstel River

Loosdrecht Lakes

Lower Rhine River

HIGH NETHERLANDS

Meuse River

Vaalser Mountain

Rhine River

IJssel River

Lake IJssel

Waddenzee

TEXEL ISLAND

WEST FRISIAN ISLANDS

GERMANY

ATLANTIC OCEAN

AFRICA

SPAIN

PORTUGAL

ITALY

UNITED KINGDOM

SWITZ.

FRANCE

LUX.

NETHERLANDS

EUROPE

500 KM

500 Miles

## Netherlands

N

Highest point

Lowest point

0        30 KM

0        30 Miles

Elevation

| Feet | Meters | |
|------|--------|---|
| 9843 | 3000 | Mountains |
| 6562 | 2000 | |
| 3281 | 1000 | Uplands |
| 1640 | 500 | |
| | | Lowlands |

LOW NETHERLANDS Located in the western and northern parts of the country, the Low Netherlands is where the Dutch battle the sea. Areas of dry land reclaimed from the sea are called polders. To make polders, people built dikes and pumped water out of wet areas. In the past, windmills pumped the water out. Modern pumps continue to do the work.

The country's approximately four thousand polders vary in size. They range from small farming plots to the huge polders that make up the province of Flevoland. The capital city, Amsterdam, and many other large cities sit on polders. The country's—and Western Europe's—lowest point is the Zuidplaspolder. It lies 22 feet (7 m) below sea level, in the west. The West Frisian Islands are an archipelago, or chain of islands, off North Holland.

The clay soil in parts of the Low Netherlands is ideal for growing crops. Productive farms are common in the region. Also present are peat bogs—large areas of vegetation that has partly decayed and packed down in layers. The dense peat provides the Dutch with fuel to burn. Farmers often graze dairy cattle on peat bogs. Some of the bogs filled with water over time and became inland lakes. The Loosdrecht Lakes, for example, are former peat bogs. They lie between the cities of Utrecht and Amsterdam.

## How Low Can You Go?

More than one-quarter (27 percent) of the Netherlands is below sea level. The nation's main airport in Amsterdam, Schiphol Airport, is almost 15 feet (4.5 m) below sea level. In 1573, before the Dutch reclaimed the land from the sea, the area was the site of a naval battle.

## ▶ Lakes and Rivers

Lakes and rivers cover about 10 percent of the Netherlands. Until 1932 a North Sea inlet covered part of the northwestern Netherlands. It formed an inland body of water called the Zuiderzee, which means "southern sea" in Dutch. In 1932 engineers blocked the sea with a 19-mile (30 km) dam. This barrier, called Afsluitdijk, formed the shallow Waddenzee and the freshwater Lake IJssel.

Three major European rivers—the Rhine, the Meuse, and the Schelde—flow into the sea at the Netherlands's coast. They enter the Netherlands in the east and south of the country and flow westward to the North Sea. The rivers are important Western European trade routes. The Rhine River is a busy waterway from Germany to the North Sea. It enters the Netherlands east of the city of Nijmegen. The Meuse arises in France and flows northward through Belgium before entering the North Sea at the Dutch port of Rotterdam. It connects

A large dam separates the North Sea *(left)* from Lake IJssel *(right)*.

industrial areas to the Rotterdam-Amsterdam-Antwerp port areas. The Schelde River runs mostly through Belgium. But its broad estuary, where the river meets the sea, is mainly in the Netherlands. The West Schelde is the Schelde's major shipping channel. Oceangoing vessels use the channel to travel between the delta area and the Belgian port of Antwerp. A branch of the Lower Rhine—the IJssel—empties into Lake IJssel.

## Climate

The climate in the Netherlands is generally mild and wet. Weather conditions are fairly uniform throughout the country. The north, however, is a little cooler than other parts of the nation.

Many winter days in the Netherlands are overcast and damp. Winter mists and fogs are common, especially in the northern and western Netherlands. Amsterdam's average temperature in January, the coldest month, is 41°F (5°C). Summers bring more comfortable temperatures. Occasional rains and cold winds also arrive from the North Sea. The capital's average temperature in July, the warmest month, is 69°F (20°C).

Rain falls regularly throughout the year. Annual rainfall throughout the country ranges between 22 and 32 inches (55 and 81 centimeters). The wettest areas lie near the coast and in the southern province of Limburg.

Storms from the North Sea strike coastal areas with full force. These powerful tempests can break through the dikes, unleashing massive floods that endanger residents and damage property. The most destructive deluge, in 1953, killed 1,850 people and destroyed thousands of homes. To prevent such damage from happening again, the Dutch built many dams and storm barriers that open and shut. These structures protect the land along all the river mouths of the delta.

## Natural Resources

For many years, the Dutch mostly burned coal for fuel. In 1959 scientists found large natural gas deposits. After the discovery, the government closed the nation's coal mines. The natural gas field in Groningen province is one of the largest in the world. Natural gas also exists in offshore fields. After workers dug wells in the 1960s in the Groningen Field, most Dutch homes and industries converted to natural gas.

The Dutch extract some petroleum (crude oil) in the southwestern province of Drenthe. Oil wells also operate offshore. They also extract oil from the floor of the North Sea. But there is not enough oil to meet the country's needs.

Land, wind, and water are other valuable resources. About 22 percent of the Netherlands's land is arable, or suitable for growing crops. Peat bogs provide fuel. Winds blow across the flatlands, and more than two thousand Dutch wind turbines harvest the power of moving air to produce electricity. Similarly, dams on rivers harness the power of rushing water to supply electricity. The nation's main rivers are important transportation routes. Fishers harvest coastal waters for herring, shrimp, and other sea life.

The nation's most abundant surface mineral is limestone. Once used as a building stone, it is more common as a component of cement and fertilizer. River valleys provide clay for bricks and roofing tiles. The Netherlands also mines salt, and sand and gravel supply construction trades.

## Flora and Fauna

Forests cover almost 11 percent of Dutch land area. Planted stands of evergreen trees account for much of the country's wooded areas. Deciduous (leaf-shedding) trees include oak, birch, beech, hornbeam, and cherry. Ashes, alders, elms, and willows thrive in areas that receive heavy rain. Various types of vegetation—ranging from heathers (evergreen shrubs) in the north to roses, linden, and buckthorn in the south—grow in the western Netherlands.

The Dutch are famous for their tulips. The flowers originally came from the Middle East. They flourish in the country's moist, spongy soil. Dutch gardeners have bred many new varieties over the centuries. In spring, tulips, crocuses, daffodils, hyacinths, and other colorful flowering plants blanket fields between the cities of Haarlem and Leiden.

**Heather** grows wild in the north of the Netherlands.

The High Netherlands is home to most of the country's wildlife. Mammals such as deer, boars, foxes, and badgers mostly survive in national parks and reserves. Red deer are protected in the Hoge Veluwe National Park, near the city of Arnhem. Pine martens live in the nation's southern and eastern areas. Southern Limburg supports some unusual fauna, including the dormouse, the midwife toad, and the wall lizard. Seals live along coastal sandbanks.

Birds love the Netherlands's wetlands. Ducks, coots, and swans paddle in the canals. Herons use their long, sharp beaks to catch tiny fish in the drainage canals around polders. Storks build large, messy nests on tall structures, including chimneys. Many migrating birds, including a dozen kinds of geese, spend winters in the country. A nature reserve near Amsterdam safeguards rare bird species, including

**A purple heron (above)** makes its summer home in the Netherlands. *Inset:* The midwife toad is one of the many unusual animals that can be found in the Netherlands.

the purple heron and many other marsh and waterbirds. Spoonbills breed on Texel Island, the largest of the West Frisian Islands.

Herring, mackerel, and plaice are among the fish that swim in coastal waters. A number of fish, including carp and eels, live in the country's canals. Perch, pike, eel, and other freshwater species populate Lake IJssel and the rivers of Zeeland province.

## Environmental Issues

The Dutch value cleanliness, and they work hard to protect their natural environment from the wear and tear of human activities. As a low-lying country, the Netherlands uses most of its hard-won land for farming, cities, and industry. Pumping water out of polders leads to sinking land and water pollution. The government buys plots of sinking farmland and lets it turn back into marshes and wetlands. Though there is little wilderness in the country, its citizens treasure their twenty national parks.

Dutch environmental laws try to limit pollution. But industries, vehicles, seawalls, and farms have a big impact on the environment. Factories, especially those that refine petroleum, create air pollution. Toxins in the air from factories fall to earth as acid rain, which can harm or kill plants. Exhaust from cars and trucks adds to the problem. Bicycles and mass transportation services such as trains are in common use and help reduce air pollution. Wind turbines are a nonpolluting energy source. But some people disapprove of them because thousands of birds die each year when they fly into the machines' huge blades.

Heavy metals from industries and fertilizer and pesticides from farm fields often pollute the nation's waters. Besides local toxins, pollution from neighboring countries also runs into the Rhine and other rivers. Water pollution has killed off many fish.

The Netherlands is vulnerable to global warming. Experts predict that this gradual rise in worldwide temperatures will raise sea levels. Impact on the low-lying Netherlands could be disastrous. The Dutch government sets aside extra money in case the low-lying country needs to strengthen and extend its protective seawalls.

### PEOPLE, PLANET, AND PROFIT

The Dutch try to balance the three Ps: people, planet, and profit. Recycling, for instance, is part of everyday life in the Netherlands. Citizens recycle half of all their household wastes and two-thirds of their glass bottles. This makes them world leaders in the effort to reduce pollution and to reuse materials.

## ▷ Cities

Most of the Dutch live in the west central Netherlands, an area of fertile land and many broad rivers. About 70 percent of the people reside in urban areas. More than 40 percent live in North and South Holland provinces, where the largest cities are Amsterdam, Rotterdam, and The Hague. The three together form an area called Randstadt.

AMSTERDAM (1.4 million population, including the larger metropolitan area) is the country's largest city and its official capital. The seat of government is in The Hague. Amsterdam was named for a dam built on the Amstel River in the 1200s, when the city was a small fishing village. In 1482 citizens walled in their coastal town to protect it from attacks and floods. In the 1500s and 1600s, Amsterdam welcomed many refugees fleeing religious persecution in other parts of Europe. They brought new skills to the city. During the Golden Age of the 1600s, the city was a leading force in European business and art.

In the twenty-first century, about 45 percent of Amsterdam's population is not Dutch-born. Home to 177 nationalities, the city has the most diverse population in the world. Housing is in short supply. Many people must live in neighborhoods outside the city limits. Factories in and around the capital produce electrical equipment, aircraft, and processed food.

Most of Amsterdam's businesses involve trade, banking, and tourism. The area near Amsterdam's Schiphol Airport is a center for many of these economic activities. In the city's Red Light District, prostitution is legal and coffee shops are allowed to sell marijuana. Tourist attractions in the city center include world-class art museums and bike paths along picturesque canals, past beautiful old buildings. Visitors can tour the Anne Frank House, where the Jewish girl Anne Frank hid from anti-Jewish German soldiers during World War II.

This aerial view of Amsterdam shows the Prinsengracht (or Prince's Canal).

The North Sea Canal links Amsterdam's harbor to the North Sea, so oceangoing vessels can enter the port. Within the city itself, shorter canals also provide access to the docks. More than one thousand bridges cross the canals. Houses that wealthy merchants built in earlier centuries line the canals.

ROTTERDAM (population 1 million, including the larger metropolitan area) is located on the Meuse River. Its huge dock facilities, called Europort, are among the busiest in the world. They handle cargo to and from the Netherlands, Germany, France, and Switzerland. A canal dug in the nineteenth century enables ships to travel from these countries to Europort and the North Sea. Oil refineries, shipyards, and banking facilities add to Rotterdam's status as a major European trading center. German bombing raids in World War II crippled Rotterdam. Urban planners rebuilt the city in the 1950s. The modern city center has shops and pedestrian malls.

THE HAGUE (population 620,000, including the larger metropolitan area) is northwest of Rotterdam. This coastal city was once the property of the counts, or nobility, of Holland. It is officially known as 's-Gravenhage, meaning "the count's hedge" (an enclosed area a count owned). In the early 1900s, the city was the site of global peace conferences. It eventually became the center of a world system of justice, home to the Permanent Court of Arbitration and the International Criminal Court. The Hague hosts the Dutch parliament and the many offices that help to run the government. The nation's monarch (king or queen) also lives and works in The Hague. The city is a hub of national and international meetings and institutions, including the United Nations. These events and organizations are central to the city's economy. The resort district of Scheveningen also brings in income from tourists and provides jobs.

UTRECHT (population 423,000, including the larger metropolitan area) lies on a branch of the Lower Rhine River. It is a major railway and highway junction. The city's residents live amid historic houses, religious buildings, and picturesque bridges. Utrecht's factories produce computer software. Workers also make more traditional goods such as cloth, musical instruments, beer, and carpets.

 Visit www.vgsbooks.com for links to websites with additional information about the many things to see and do in the Netherlands and its weather, plants, and animals.

# HISTORY AND GOVERNMENT

People lived in the area that became the Netherlands as many as 250,000 years ago. Prehistoric stone tools from that era are the earliest signs of human habitation. Scientists have also found burial mounds from about 3000 B.C. Made out of huge stones, the grave sites contain artifacts of an early civilization.

In the 50s B.C., the Roman Empire, based in Rome, Italy, expanded northward. Led by Julius Caesar, the Roman army made contact with people called the Belgae. They lived south of the Rhine, in the present-day southern Netherlands and northern Belgium. Germanic groups named the Batavi and the Frisians dwelt in the northern Netherlands.

By 15 B.C., the Romans had conquered the lands of the Belgae. They added their new territory to the Roman province of Gaul (modern France). Rome treated the Batavi as allies who could supply soldiers for Roman armies. The Romans failed to push north of the Rhine into the lands of the Frisians. In this wet area, the inhabitants built homes on terps, or islands of earth, to be safe from floodwaters.

## The Franks

In the next four hundred years, the Romans built towns, farms, and roads in northern Europe. In the fourth century, Roman power was fading and they began to pull out of their northern strongholds. In the early 400s, a Germanic group called the Franks moved into Roman areas. Successful in most of their conquests, the Franks could not overcome the fierce and stubborn Frisians. They continued to follow their own laws and religious practices.

By the end of the seventh century, the Franks controlled most of the Netherlands except for the Frisian lands. The Franks spread their Christian religion in the Netherlands.

The Frisians defied Frankish power and kept control of much of the seacoast into the 700s. They built earthen walls around the ancient terps to protect them from the sea. Frisian windmills pumped water out of the encircled land. These Frisian efforts led to the Dutch tradition of polder building.

This drawing from the fourteenth century shows **the coronation of Emperor Charlemagne by Pope Leo III** in the ninth century.

By the late 700s, however, the Frankish ruler Charlemagne had conquered the Frisian lands. He made them part of his large kingdom. His realm had the backing of the pope, the head of the Christian church, based in Rome.

After Charlemagne's death in 814, his heirs divided the Frankish Empire among themselves. During the next one hundred years, the Netherlands passed into the hands of several rulers. In 925 the East Frankish Kingdom (modern Germany) gained control of the Netherlands, which had come to be called Lorraine.

## The Rise of Cities

During the ninth and tenth centuries, the people of Lorraine faced devastating floods. They also faced attacks by Vikings—raiders from farther north in Scandinavia. Far from the center of German government, the people received little help in their struggles. Local lords felt only a weak loyalty to the German emperor. They assembled crews to build more polders and dikes in the 1100s.

German power in Lorraine was greatest in Utrecht. The emperor had a home in the city. Elsewhere in the region, dukes and counts built castles near the mouths of important rivers. Traders and craftspeople settled near the castles for protection. In the thirteenth and fourteenth centuries, such communities grew in size and importance. Charters, or legal contracts, between local lords and these communities set taxation, military service, and other laws.

The chartered cities organized water councils to watch the polders, dikes, and canals closely. The water councils repaired or strengthened them, as needed. The growing settlements also developed local industries and founded guilds. The guilds were associations of merchants and craftspeople. Trade was essential. Ships carried wood, wine, metals, spices, and coal to many places inland and along the coast.

Coastal towns prospered. They built fleets of trading ships and established their own governments. Some cities grew powerful by joining the Hanseatic League. This was a business group that began in Germany. The league attempted to standardize trading customs and to protect merchant ships and towns from pirates. The league also tried to set commercial laws and to gain new trading privileges for its members.

## Burgundian Rule

Local leaders fought many small, internal wars. In the mid-1300s, five nobles emerged as the most powerful leaders in the Netherlands. These nobles set up local governments, called estates. Knights, merchants, religious clergy, and craftspeople could participate in the estates. Members of the various estates served on committees. The nobles needed the estates' approval to raise money through taxes.

In 1419 Philip, the Duke of Burgundy in France became the Count of Flanders (located mostly in modern Belgium). He began to expand his holdings through inheritance, purchase, politics, and war. In the northern lowlands, rich merchants welcomed Burgundian rule. They saw it as a way to ensure law and order, which would help commerce.

In the south, however, the wealthy trading towns of Brugge and Ghent (in present-day Belgium) resisted this threat to their independence. Revolts occurred in the mid-1400s. But Philip was determined to unite the lowlands under his authority. By the late 1450s, he had taken control of these chartered towns and limited their self-government.

To centralize his authority, Philip gathered representatives from his various holdings in 1465. Meeting in Brussels (the capital of Belgium), this assembly marked the beginning of the Dutch parliament, called the States-General. Philip also appointed a council to oversee the lowlands' legal and financial matters.

This sixteenth-century French painting shows **Philip, the Duke of Burgundy,** who was known as Philip the Good.

Philip's son and successor, Charles the Bold, further strengthened the central government. He created a permanent army and expanded his territory. His aggression angered his neighbors in Germany, France, and Switzerland. They declared war on Charles, who died in battle in 1477.

Nineteen-year-old Mary of Burgundy, Charles's only child, inherited his rule. After Charles's defeat, France seized Burgundy. Amid this turmoil, representatives of several provinces in the Netherlands forced Mary to sign a treaty. It gave important powers back to local Dutch governments. In return, local leaders pledged to continue to help pay for Mary's war against France.

## The Habsburgs

Soon after her father's death, Mary married Archduke Maximilian of Habsburg. The Habsburgs ruled the Holy Roman Empire. The empire covered much of central Europe. With the military help of the Habsburgs, Mary kept her territories in the Netherlands. After her death in 1482, Maximilian governed her lands in the name of their young son, Philip, Duke of Burgundy.

In the late 1480s and early 1490s, the Burgundians sought to keep control of rich Dutch towns and their trade. The various regions of the Netherlands resisted Burgundian rule, but Maximilian held on to the valuable territory.

Through the Habsburgs, the Burgundians had a strong ally in the Roman Catholic Church. But in the late 1400s, some people believed the church was misusing its power. The Dutch philosopher Desiderius Erasmus was one of the critics. Through his writings, Erasmus pressed for changes in corrupt church practices and unwise political ties. He felt they conflicted with Christian teachings.

In 1496 Philip married Joan, the daughter and heir of the king of Spain. By 1519 their son, Emperor Charles V, had inherited Spain, the Burgundian realm (including the Netherlands), and all the Habsburg lands. Charles expanded the Netherlands northward either by purchase or by conquest.

Charles gave his attention to other parts of his large empire. He appointed representatives, called stadtholders (placeholders), to run the many provinces in the Netherlands and Belgium. Although they had some powers, stadtholders were not royalty. They met in Brussels to discuss taxes and to direct day-to-day affairs.

## Reformation and Revolution

Throughout these centuries of growth and shifting loyalties, the people of the Netherlands remained loyal to the Roman Catholic branch of Christianity. Erasmus and other writers tried to point out the need for church reforms. Protests against church policy led to the Protestant Reformation, which challenged the church's authority.

Protestant ideas first spread to the Netherlands in the 1500s. The strict Protestant preacher John Calvin urged hard work and simple tastes. In response to Calvin's activities, Charles V encouraged the Roman Catholic Church to execute people suspected of heresy (opposition to Catholic teachings). Religious persecution increased, but Protestant ideas took firm root in the northern Netherlands. Provinces there also united to express their dissatisfaction with Charles's rule.

Charles was weary of his long reign and disillusioned by the widespread opposition. He gave up his throne in 1555. Discontent worsened under the reign of his son and successor, Philip II. Philip ruled both Spain and the Netherlands. He had grown up in Spain with little understanding of Dutch culture. He stationed Spanish troops and government workers on Dutch territory. He also taxed the Dutch to pay for Spain's wars against France.

To strengthen the Catholic Church, Philip gave more land in the Netherlands to Catholic bishops (church officials). He also authorized an inquisition, or church trial, against Calvinists. Dutch nobles and commoners alike suffered imprisonment, expulsion (being forced to leave the country), and execution because of their beliefs. To avoid arrest, thousands of Dutch Calvinists fled the country.

Hurt by oppressive policies, heavy taxes, and soaring food prices, the people began to rebel. They rioted and destroyed Roman Catholic

**Dutch citizens destroy Roman Catholic Church property in April 1566.** This engraving is by Frans Hogenberg.

property. In response, Philip sent ten thousand troops under the Duke of Alva to crush the rebellions. The duke ordered the execution of thousands.

In 1568 William I, Prince of Orange, led the nobles in a Dutch revolt against Philip II. It was the beginning of what became known as the Dutch War of Independence (1568–1648). Both Dutch Catholics and Dutch Calvinists fought the Spanish. Another group of nobles pleaded with Spanish officials to stop the Inquisition, to allow religious freedom, and to assemble the States-General. One of Philip's advisers called these noble petitioners "beggars." As a revolutionary movement grew, its backers adopted this name.

Spanish armies controlled most Dutch towns. By 1572, however, William of Orange had gathered a group of rebels who operated from England. Known as the Sea Beggars, they attacked Spanish ships and raided coastal towns. Within a short time, the Sea Beggars had captured the provinces (counties) of Zeeland and Holland. Dutch cities began to defy Spanish authorities openly.

The Duke of Alva fought back with land forces. They inflicted great damage in other parts of the Netherlands. But the country's geography—with its hard-to-cross bogs, rivers, and lakes—made overland travel difficult. The terrain stopped the Spanish from quickly striking the Dutch. In 1573 the Sea Beggars defeated Alva's fleet on the Zuiderzee. Afterward, Philip called the duke back to Spain.

## ▶ Religious Divisions

Although Catholics and Protestants joined forces to fight the Spaniards, religion still divided the Dutch. Most Dutch Catholics lived in the southern provinces. Dutch Calvinists were mainly in the north. William persuaded members of the States-General in Brussels to set aside their religious differences and to unite against Spanish rule. The members signed the Pacification (Peace) of Ghent in 1576. The document called for religious freedom in the Netherlands. The next year, representatives signed the Union of Brussels. This document unified the provinces.

In 1577 the provinces all voted to reject the new Spanish governor—John of Austria—unless Philip agreed to withdraw all Spanish forces and to accept Dutch demands for religious freedom. To avoid further warfare, Philip consented to these conditions.

Unity among the Dutch was short-lived, however. Southern leaders didn't trust the Dutch Calvinists. Northern leaders distrusted the southerners' ties to Spanish Catholics. Alessandro Farnese succeeded John as governor. He urged the southern Catholics to withdraw from the Union of Brussels, offering them Spanish protection. As a result, three southern provinces (present-day Belgium) declared their loyalty to Catholicism and to Philip in 1579.

In the same year, seven northern provinces, including Holland, broke with Spain. They signed the Declaration of Utrecht, promising to defend liberty and freedom of religion. In 1581 the northern

## THE CARROT OF ORANGE

Before the 1500s, carrots tasted bitter and were white, pale purple, or yellow. Then Dutch growers began to breed an orange carrot, which was a variation of the yellow carrot. According to a popular legend, the carrot's color honors William of Orange, the hero of Dutch independence. Historians, however, believe the gardeners developed the orange vegetable because it was sweeter than the yellow. (The chemical beta-carotene gives carrots their orange color and also adds health benefits.) The Dutch orange carrot is the ancestor of everyday modern carrots.

Catholics unwilling to sign the Pacification of Ghent are forced from Antwerp (which was part of the Netherlands) in 1578. This engraving is by Frans Hogenberg.

provinces declared themselves independent. This was the beginning of the Netherlands as a separate political unit. The new nation, called the United Provinces of the Netherlands, had no single head of state. Zeeland and Holland, the two richest provinces of the new union, appointed William of Orange as the first stadtholder of the new territory. It operated as a republic—ruled by the people, not a monarch. The Dutch believed people should control their own lives. They did not consider William their king.

## Independence and Trade

Spain did not accept the new, independent union. Spain battled the United Provinces on land and at sea. The Dutch continued their fight for independence even after a Catholic extremist assassinated William in 1584. William's son, Maurice, took over for his father and led a number of successful battles on land. The Dutch also won sea battles against the Spanish.

Portuguese ships had long brought spices, silks, and other goods from Southeast Asia into Dutch ports. But then Spain took over Portugal. After the Spanish takeover, Dutch merchants had to find new suppliers of these imports. In 1602 the merchants formed the Dutch East India Company to trade directly with Asian countries. The Dutch government gave this private company the power to make treaties with Asian rulers. It also allowed the use of military force to promote trade. Within a few years, the Dutch had replaced the Portuguese as the leading traders and colonizers in Southeast Asia. The Dutch also

**Ships of the Dutch East India Company** sail into Amsterdam. This mosaic is made of Delft tiles.

became the fourth-leading transporters of enslaved Africans, in the Atlantic slave trade. Dutch merchants bought and shipped humans from Africa mostly to the New World of the Americas.

The Dutch East India Company thrived. Dutch merchants pursued their goals ruthlessly. Sometimes they killed people who refused to sell their goods to the company. In Southeast Asia, the Dutch pushed the Portuguese out of Ceylon (modern Sri Lanka) and parts of present-day Malaysia and Indonesia. With their wealth of spices and woods, the almost three thousand Indonesian islands became the jewel in the Dutch Empire. The Dutch East Indies colonies relied on slaves from Asia for laborers.

The Dutch West India Company was founded in 1621. It acquired territory in Brazil and in Dutch Guiana (present-day Suriname) in South America. The Dutch West Indies colonies in this area relied on African slave labor.

Trade flourished during lulls in the fight for independence from Spain. It did especially well in the province of Holland and its main port at Amsterdam. Among the most profitable items were tiles and other earthenware goods made in the Dutch city of Delft. The blue and white Delft pottery imitated fine Chinese porcelain. It became popular throughout Europe.

In 1609 Spain and the United Provinces signed a truce. But by 1621, the war had broken out again. It became part of a larger conflict in Europe known as the Thirty Years' War (1618–1648). The Dutch—with the French as allies—struggled, with limited success, to take over Flanders.

In 1648 the Thirty Years' War—and the Dutch War of Independence—ended with the signing of the Peace of Westphalia. Under the peace treaty's terms, Spain recognized the Netherlands as a free, self-ruling state. Spain also gave the Dutch the Caribbean islands of the Netherlands Antilles and Aruba.

## TULIP FEVER

In the mid-1600s, the Dutch were swept up in a passion for tulips. The middle classes had become so rich that they spent huge amounts of money on luxuries. Wealthy merchants turned their homes into little palaces and began to decorate their gardens with tulips. Flower growers cultivated tulips to create fantastic new colors and forms. Rare tulip bulbs were sold for outlandish prices. Records show that one bulb was traded for six carts of grain, four oxen, twelve sheep, two casks of wine, four casks of beer, 1,000 pounds (454 kilograms) of cheese, a dress, and a silver goblet. The government finally stepped in and put an end to the extreme prices, which were creating social disorder as people went into debt to buy tulips.

# The Golden Age

Despite the many wars of the seventeenth century, the Netherlands enjoyed great prosperity. Wealth flowed into the country from its growing empire. In the mid-1600s, Amsterdam became the financial capital of Europe. Leiden became a famous center of learning. Dutch culture and art, particularly painting, flourished during this Golden Age. The Dutch also drained more polders to expand farmlands.

**William III, Prince of Orange**

To protect their wealth and trade interests, the Dutch became involved in several foreign wars. The French and the English allied in 1670 to destroy Dutch commercial power. In 1672 Dutch forces under Johan de Witt failed to protect several towns from French attacks. In response, the Orangists revolted. As the French advanced, a mob murdered Johan de Witt. The States-General made William III, Prince of Orange, stadtholder. The States-General hoped he could stop the French.

Under William's leadership, the Dutch opened the dikes and flooded the western lowlands to push the French out. The Dutch navy defeated the English at sea. After a series of battles, however, the Dutch lost its North American colonies to the English. William regained lost territory before making peace with England in 1674 and with France in 1678.

William's wife, Mary, was the heir to the English throne. In 1689 the two became joint rulers of England. At this time, England was fighting the French king Louis XIV as he tried to expand his territory and power. As King of England and the stadtholder of the Netherlands, William stood strong against France.

Orange is the Netherlands's national color and fruit. Originally the color and the fruit had nothing to do with the name of the House of Orange-Nassau, which the Dutch royal family belongs to. Their ancestors used to own an area in France called Orange. The place-name comes from an ancient water god called Arausio. William I was the Count of Nassau, in Germany, and held the title Prince of Orange. The Dutch word for the color orange is *oranje*. The Dutch word for the fruit, however, is *sinaasappel*, or *appelsien*, which means "Chinese apples."

# From Republic to Monarchy

During the eighteenth century, the Dutch economy declined. Other European merchants improved their foreign trade. They bought fewer goods from Dutch brokers. Amsterdam lost some of its importance as Europe's trading center. Government corruption drained funds meant to improve the economy. Costly wars against Prussia (in modern Germany) and France in the mid-1700s and against Britain in the 1780s took the lives of many Dutch.

In 1795 France occupied the entire country. In 1806 the French ruler and general Napoleon Bonaparte declared the Netherlands, still occupied by France, a kingdom. He made his brother Louis the king. French rule in the Netherlands weakened the merchant families. Therefore, the Dutch government, which had become centralized, was able to claim more power. The state took over the Dutch East India Company. It took education out of the hands of local authorities.

Napoleon continued to attempt to conquer Europe for France. The major European powers came together to stop him. Defeats in 1813 forced Napoleon to withdraw French troops from the Netherlands.

## WIN SOME, LOSE SOME

In 1621 the Dutch West India Company started a colony in North America called New Netherland. Its capital was New Amsterdam, on the island of Manhattan. In 1624 the colony's governor, Peter Minuit, bought Manhattan from local Native Americans. He paid in goods worth 60 Dutch guilders (about $24), or about $.05 per acre ($.02 per hectare). It was a great investment. In the twenty-first century, land in Manhattan sells for about $827,000 per acre ($330,800 per hectare). The Dutch never got a return on their money though. In 1674 they lost their colony to the British, who changed New Amsterdam's name to New York.

# The 1800s

The European alliance finally defeated Napoleon in 1815. The victors held a postwar meeting called the Congress of Vienna. At the meeting, they added Belgium and Luxembourg, which had also been under French control, to the Netherlands. The allies hoped that a large Kingdom of the Netherlands would help stop the French from regaining power.

The Dutch set up a constitutional monarchy, with a king or queen to head the country and a constitution to guide the country's lawmakers. Dutch leaders invited the Prince of Orange—a descendant of William of Orange—to become King William I. A new constitution created a two-house legislature.

William I improved his country's economy by building new waterways. He also established tariffs, or taxes on imports, to protect Dutch goods from competition. The Dutch government took control of the Dutch East Indies (in modern Indonesia) from the failing Dutch East India Company. In 1819 the Netherlands abolished the slave trade—though not the practice of slavery in its colonies.

The Belgians did not approve of William. They especially disliked the Calvinist king's efforts to control their Roman Catholic schools. Because of their dissatisfaction, Belgians revolted in August 1830 and drove Dutch troops from Brussels. William accepted Belgian independence in 1839. Belgium received part of Luxembourg. The remaining part became the Grand Duchy of Luxembourg. A duchy is a territory under the rule of a duke. Luxembourg recognized King William as grand duke.

In 1840 William I announced plans to marry a Catholic. In response, the Dutch forced him to give up his throne. In the following decades, liberal movements prompted the Dutch government to change the nation's constitution.

The change reduced the monarch's powers and guaranteed freedom of the press, of assembly, and of religion. The States-General received greater lawmaking powers, and more people could vote. Other changes affected trade and working conditions. For example, a canal linking the port of Rotterdam to the North Sea improved trade. Workers formed labor unions, and new laws legalized strikes (work stoppages

**Dutch troops withdraw from Brussels in 1830.** This engraving is by Belgian artist Paulus Lauters.

designed to pressure employers to meet workers' demands). In 1863 laws abolished slavery in Dutch colonies.

To lessen conflict between Roman Catholics and Protestants, the Dutch established *verzuiling*. The word means "columning." Under verzuiling, different religious organizations ran separate schools, clubs, political parties, newspapers, and radio stations for their members.

King William III died in 1890. His ten-year-old daughter, Wilhelmina, succeeded him. Luxembourg's laws prevented females from inheriting the grand duchy. Thus Luxembourg ended its union with the Netherlands and became an independent state.

## ▷ The World Wars

The Netherlands did not take sides during World War I (1914–1918). The conflict pitted the allied nations of Britain, France, and Russia against Germany and Austria. The Netherlands's unsafe location between the warring Allies and Germans, however, made it hard for the Dutch to stay neutral. German submarine attacks severely damaged Dutch ships, and the Allies took over the Dutch merchant fleet. The Dutch drafted 450,000 troops to protect the nation's borders.

Social reforms began again after the war. New laws established a shorter, eight-hour workday and other improvements for workers. The legislature also granted voting rights to all men in 1917 and to women in 1919. In 1929 the Netherlands and many other nations agreed to reject war when they signed the Kellogg-Briand Pact.

**Dutch troops guard the Dutch-Belgian border** during World War I. The Netherlands tried to stay neutral but found it necessary to defend its borders due to its strategic location in Europe.

## THE LAW OF PEACE

Dutch lawyer Tobias Asser (1838–1913) was a spokesperson for world peace. He believed that laws and meetings were the best way to solve global conflicts. In 1911 Asser won the Nobel Peace Prize for helping to create the Permanent Court of Arbitration (PCA). Arbitration is a way of settling differences, in which two or more people or groups agree to accept the decision of a neutral third party. A building called the Peace Palace in The Hague houses the PCA, along with the United Nations' International Court of Justice.

A worldwide economic depression in the 1930s led to hardships and insecurity for many people. These problems contributed to the growth of strict regimes in some parts of Europe. In neighboring Germany, for example, Adolf Hitler and his Nazi Party gained power. Some Dutch extremists agreed with the Nazi's harsh measures to restore social and economic stability.

While the Nazis began to take over territories on the European continent, the Netherlands stayed neutral. The country did, however, call up its military forces. In August 1939, Queen Wilhelmina offered her services as a negotiator in the hope of avoiding another global conflict. But Germany's invasion of Poland in September led Britain and France to declare war.

Nazi Germany launched land and air assaults on the Netherlands. On May 10, 1940, Germany bombed central Rotterdam. Within hours, tens of thousands of buildings were rubble. The Dutch army surrendered to Germany on

**Rotterdam crumbled under German bombardment** in May 1940.

May 14. Queen Wilhelmina and her ministers fled to Britain. There, they formed a government in exile. The Dutch navy and merchant fleet escaped and were able to help the Allies (Britain and other countries fighting Nazi Germany).

German troops occupied the Netherlands and set up a pro-Nazi government. A minority of Dutch people belonged to the NSB (National Socialist Movement), which supported the Germans. As the war progressed, Dutch from all walks of life formed an underground (secret) resistance movement. The Germans executed Dutch citizens in return. They forced thousands of Dutch prisoners to toil in labor camps.

Throughout the territories they conquered, the Nazis imprisoned and killed Jews and other people they considered "undesirable." They sent most Dutch Jews to their deaths, mostly in the Auschwitz extermination center. Non-Jewish civilians resisted by hiding Jews. One young Jew, Anne Frank, recorded her experiences in a diary. Her father found and published it after her death at the end of the war.

The Germans refitted Dutch factories for their own use and seized local food supplies. Many people starved. In the final months of the war, the Allied troops bombed the Netherlands to help force a German defeat. Nazi troops retreated from the country. As they left, they destroyed dikes, flooding vast areas. In 1945 Germany surrendered.

## Postwar Recovery

After the war, large loans from other countries helped the Dutch to rebuild their factories, repair their cities, and strengthen their sea barriers. Massive flooding had ruined Dutch farmland. The Netherlands avoided famine by buying food from abroad.

Postwar Dutch governments wanted the Netherlands to be involved in international affairs. The country became a founding member of the United Nations in 1945. It set up a trade association with Belgium and Luxembourg. In 1949 the Netherlands joined the North Atlantic Treaty Organization (NATO), a defensive military alliance of Western European nations and the United States.

Meanwhile, Dutch governments were facing difficult problems overseas. After the war ended, many Dutch colonies in Southeast Asia demanded self-rule. Fierce fighting between local peoples and Dutch troops occurred in Java, Sumatra, parts of Borneo, Sulawesi, and the Moluccas—all in Southeast Asia. In 1949 the Dutch government recognized the independence of these territories. They later formed the Republic of Indonesia. The Netherlands eventually gave up its other colonies in Asia and most of its South American holdings as well.

Back at home, disaster struck on February 1, 1953. On that day, the North Sea surged into the delta area during a heavy storm. Severe

In February 1953, **massive floods destroyed Oude-Tonge** and many other villages in the delta area of the Netherlands.

flooding killed 1,850 people. In response, Dutch engineers built an extensive system of dams, known as the Delta Project.

In 1957 Belgium, the Netherlands, and Luxembourg—together called the Benelux nations—became members of the Common Market. This large European organization promoted trade and economic unity among its member nations. It evolved over time into the European Community (EC).

## New Concerns and a New Queen

Dutch industries grew rapidly in the 1960s and 1970s. New facilities for refining and storing oil made Rotterdam a major petroleum distribution center. The success of Dutch industry brought new challenges. Environmental problems worsened as industries released harmful wastes into the water, air, and soil. When oil-producing Arab states raised the price of petroleum in the 1970s, the Dutch economy, which relied on foreign oil, fell. The government also ran into problems paying for wide-ranging social benefits to Dutch citizens. In increasing numbers, Dutch workers began to rely on welfare benefits for their income instead of working.

In the 1970s and 1980s, social concerns grew, particularly among Dutch young people. Political activists protested the Netherlands's role in NATO and the country's housing shortage and water pollution. In some cases, the protesters successfully blocked projects that threatened the environment. When the Dutch colony of Suriname became independent in 1975, hundreds of thousands of Surinamese moved to the Netherlands. Another hundred thousand people from Turkey and Morocco also moved to the Netherlands to work. The immigrants were mostly Muslims, who follow the religion of Islam. They came as temporary guest workers, but most stayed and brought their families to the country. The face of Dutch society began to change.

In 1980 Queen Wilhelmina stepped down, and her daughter Beatrix became queen. Two years later, Ruud Lubbers began a long term as prime minister after promising to improve the economy. Lubbers cut spending on some welfare programs. He also halted plans to build or repair roads, railways, and canals. Plans to expand schools and hospitals ground to a halt.

Despite the loss of some government services, most Dutch supported Lubbers's actions. The policies slowed rising prices, stimulated businesses, and created new jobs. The government's cutbacks, however, did not affect the completion of the Delta Project. Queen Beatrix officially opened it in 1986.

In 1993 a group of European nations, including the Netherlands, formed the European Union. Member nations agreed to unite their markets so that people, trade goods, services, and money could move freely across borders. The union's goal was to strengthen the European economy and to reduce tensions among nations.

Floods again hit the country hard in 1995. Serious flooding drove a quarter million people out of their homes.

*Left:* Ruud Lubbers was prime minister from 1982 to 1994. *Right:* Queen Beatrix, pictured in 2009, became queen of the Netherlands in 1980.

# The Twenty-first Century

In 2000 the Netherlands confirmed its reputation of being socially liberal, or open to different ways of living—and dying. The country became the first in the world to legalize euthanasia (painlessly ending a life, to relieve the suffering of a dying person). Doctors who assist in a person's death must follow strict rules. Same-sex marriage also became legal that year.

After the September 11, 2001, terrorist attacks in the United States, the Netherlands sent troops to Afghanistan to try to destroy the terrorist organization al-Qaeda. The next year saw major changes to the Netherlands. The country replaced the Dutch guilder with the euro, the EU's common currency. In May the first murder of a Dutch politician since the 1600s rocked Dutch society. Dutchman and animal-rights activist Volkert van der Graaf shot and killed politician Pim Fortuyn. In the twenty-first century, more Muslim immigrants had arrived from Islamic countries such as Somalia. They added to the many Muslims who had come to the Netherlands in the mid-twentieth century. Fortuyn had frequently spoken out against the influx of Muslim immigrants, saying they were destroying Dutch culture. The murderer believed that Fortuyn's views were a threat to democracy.

Dutch society's long tradition of tolerance took another blow in 2004. Dutch-born Mohammed Bouyeri shot and killed filmmaker Theo van Gogh as he bicycled to work. The filmmaker had criticized Islamic treatment of women, in his short film *Submission*. Bouyeri, a Muslim whose father had come from Morocco, left a note on van Gogh's body saying he was an enemy of Islam. The murder shocked the world and heightened ethnic tension in the Netherlands. It became known as the Dutch September 11, in reference to the terrorist attacks in the United States. Afterward, the Dutch government passed laws strictly limiting immigration. In 2005 parliament ruled that immigrants must pass a test in Dutch language and culture before they are permitted to live in the country.

The next year, 1,400 Dutch troops joined NATO-led forces in Afghanistan. Jan Peter Balkenende became prime minister in 2007. He headed a coalition (power-sharing arrangement) of three political parties. A worldwide financial crisis began to hurt the Dutch economy in 2008. Because the Netherlands is a major player in global trade, its economy went into a decline for the first time in decades.

The rise in ethnic tensions and the recession (economic downturn) put stresses on Dutch society. In 2009 a man drove into a crowd gathered in Apeldoorn to greet Queen Beatrix and her family. The driver killed seven people and himself. Before he died, he told police that he was protesting the loss of his job.

Early in 2010, Prime Minister Balkenende resigned over disagreements about whether or not to withdraw troops from Afghanistan. The Dutch soldiers served in peaceful roles, such as training police and overseeing roadwork. The war-torn country iss deadly for foreign troops, however, and twenty-one Dutch soldiers have been killed there.

## ⊙ Government

The Netherlands is a constitutional monarchy. The constitution outlines the structure of the government. The queen or king fills a symbolic role. The country is a democracy, and all citizens eighteen and older are eligible to vote.

The executive branch consists of the monarch; the prime minister; and a cabinet, or group of advisers. The monarch appoints the prime minister, who heads the government. He or she usually comes from the political party with the most seats in the parliament. The prime minister appoints the cabinet.

The legislative branch is a bicameral, or two-house, parliament, called the States-General. Provincial councils (elected by citizens) elect 75 ministers to the upper house, the First Chamber. They serve six-year terms. Dutch citizens vote for the 150 deputies of the lower house, the Second Chamber. The deputies serve four-year terms. The States-General must approve each bill before it becomes a law.

In the Netherlands, 37 percent of representatives in parliament are women.

The Dutch judicial branch is independent. All judges serve for life. There are no trials by jury. The Supreme Court has twenty-six members. It can strike down decisions of lower courts. The judiciary also includes courts of appeal, district courts, and subdistrict courts. A national ombudsman (investigator) looks into disagreements between the government and citizens. The lower house appoints the ombudsman to a six-year term.

The twelve provinces of the Netherlands are similar to counties. The people elect a local council to run their province. Each provincial council names an executive to administer daily duties.

The Netherlands Antilles and Aruba are also part of the Kingdom of the Netherlands. These islands in the Caribbean have their own cabinet ministers and governors. They report to lawmaking bodies elected by the citizens.

Visit www.vgsbooks.com for links to websites with more about the history and government of the Netherlands.

# THE PEOPLE

The Netherlands is home to 16.5 million people. With an average population density of 1,035 people per square mile (400 per sq. km), the country is one of Europe's most crowded nations. The average Dutch birthrate is 1.8 children per woman. The population is growing at a slow rate of 0.3 percent, counting new immigrants. If this growth holds steady, experts predict the population will reach 17.2 million by 2025.

With 66 percent of the population living in cities, many Dutch urban areas face housing shortages and a heavy load on services. With so many people in such a small area, the Dutch long ago realized the importance of careful urban planning.

The Dutch generally admire honesty, hard work, modesty, a sense of humor, and good education. They also take a liberal view of human behavior. This open attitude has led to laws allowing same-sex marriage and a sex workers (prostitution) industry. The sale of so-called soft (nonlethal) drugs such as marijuana is tolerated. The Netherlands was the first country in the world to allow doctors to legally help suffering people end their lives.

## Health and Welfare

The Dutch value social equality. They choose to pay high taxes to support a welfare system so that all citizens receive social services. The state provides health and dental insurance for all low-income citizens. Families with children receive allowances, as do widows and orphans. Retirement benefits are generous. All Dutch who are unemployed for any reason receive funds that equal a percentage of their former wages.

In previous decades, as unemployment benefits grew more plentiful, so did the number of Dutch workers claiming to be sick or disabled. In the early 1990s, one-fourth of Amsterdam's residents were living on welfare benefits. Growing absenteeism and tougher educational requirements for new jobs caused labor shortages and unemployment in the Dutch economy. The government took major steps in the twenty-first century to reform the very expensive welfare system. In 2003 the government trimmed the welfare budget. Stricter guidelines govern who can receive benefits.

The Dutch benefit from an excellent system of health care. A key indicator of the health of the country is its infant mortality rate (IMR), or the number of babies who die before they are one year old. The Netherlands's IMR of 4 babies per 1,000 live births is one of the world's best rates. The average life expectancy of a baby born in the Netherlands is 80 years. In comparison, the average life expectancy in Suriname is 70 years. Pregnant Dutchwomen face a very low 1 in 10,200 chance of dying in childbirth-related causes.

As in other industrialized countries, the major health risks in the Netherlands are heart disease and cancer. Poor stress management and unhealthy lifestyle choices (such as smoking cigarettes and eating high-fat diets) are other health concerns.

The Dutch approach to drug addiction is to send addicts to treatment centers. The state also provides clean needles for drug users to prevent the spread of the HIV virus that causes AIDS. The virus spreads through body fluids, including blood, which often remains in needles after injections. The rate of HIV/AIDS infection in the Netherlands is a low 0.2 percent of the adult population.

Private organizations operate most health-care facilities in the Netherlands, and a number are still associated with churches. Medical costs are paid through government or private health insurance companies. Home nursing organizations provide health care for the elderly, for pregnant women, and for children.

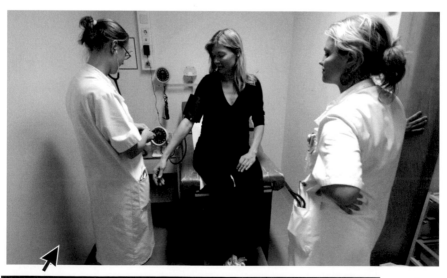

**A pregnant woman receives a checkup at a hospital in Amsterdam.** The Dutch have an excellent health-care system, especially for expectant mothers.

Euthanasia is legal in the Netherlands. Doctors who assist people to end their lives painlessly must follow a long list of strict guidelines. The person must be in unbearable suffering, with no hope of improvement. He or she must clearly, voluntarily, and repeatedly request death. About 2 percent of all deaths in the Netherlands each year are assisted. Most of the people who choose euthanasia are dying of painful cancer. Abortion is also legal in the Netherlands. With ample sex education and health care, however, the Dutch abortion rate is among the lowest in the world.

## Ethnic and Social Traits

Members of ethnic groups share cultural practices, language, and traditions. In the modern Netherlands, 81 percent of the people belong to the Dutch ethnic group. They are the descendants of several European groups: Celts, Germans, Franks, and Vikings. The Celtic and Germanic peoples were the first known inhabitants of the Netherlands. The Franks began moving into the area in the fifth century A.D. In the ninth century, Vikings from Denmark intermarried with the population. The Dutch ethnic group is a mixture of all of these peoples.

Immigrants from other parts of the European Union make up 5 percent of the population. People from Italy and Spain make up the largest percent of EU immigrants. They first came to the Netherlands in the 1960s, when the Dutch economy badly needed workers.

Workers from Turkey and Morocco also began to come to the country in the 1960s. In the twenty-first century, the Turkish and Moroccan ethnic groups each make up about 2 percent of Dutch society. They often live in neighborhoods with other members of the same ethnic group. The young people in these groups tend to marry people of the same ethnic group.

## THE TALL PERSON'S CLUB

On average, the Dutch are the tallest people in the world. The height of the average Dutchman is 6 feet 1 inch (1.8 m). The average woman is 5 feet 7 inches (1.7 m) tall. There is even a Dutch Tall Person's Club that calls attention to their need for things like longer beds and taller bikes. People who study human height are called auxologists. They point out that besides genetics, health and diet are key factors in height. Pregnant women and infants in the Netherlands receive excellent medical care. This is a cornerstone of the nation's good health and contributes to its citizens' exceptional height. Further, because the Dutch enjoy a strong economy, everybody can afford nourishing food.

## THE DUTCH

In their own language, Dutch people call themselves Nederlanders and their language Nederlands. *Dutch* comes from the old German word "duutsch," which means "of the people." Originally it referred to the language of all German and Dutch peoples. It began to mean the language and people of the Netherlands around 1600, after the Dutch established a unified, independent nation. The English enemies of the Dutch used the word as an insult. A "Dutch treat," for instance, is one you have to pay for yourself.

In the twentieth century, immigrants from former Dutch colonies arrived in the Netherlands. They mainly came from Indonesia and Suriname. Each group represents about 2 percent of Dutch society.

Indonesians came to the Netherlands after the colony won independence in 1949. They have mostly assimilated (fit in) well into Dutch society. Suriname is on the Caribbean coast of South America. Its culture is more like other Caribbean countries than other South American cultures. Almost as many Surinamese people (328,300) live in the Netherlands as in Suriname (494,000). The country became independent of the Netherlands in 1975. Dutch remains its official language, so immigrants to the Netherlands speak the

**Indonesian women beat drums in a festival procession** in Brunssum, a city in the southeastern Netherlands. Indonesians are one of the largest immigrant groups in the Netherlands.

language. The two largest ethnic groups are the Indo-Surinamese (of southern Asian ancestry) and Afro-Surinamese (of African ancestry). People from the Netherlands Antilles and Aruba make up 1 percent of the Netherlands. Another 5 percent of the Dutch population comes from many places around the world.

The Netherlands has a reputation for tolerance of different cultures and religions. For example, during the 1500s and 1600s, Jews from many parts of Europe and French Protestants called Huguenots fled to the Netherlands to seek freedom from religious persecution. This history also explains why some Dutch Christians risked their lives to protect Jews from Nazi abuse during World War II. The Dutch national television network broadcasts in Turkish, Arabic, Italian, and other languages.

Ethnic minorities in the Netherlands have higher unemployment rates and lower incomes than the Dutch ethnic group. More than 40 percent of immigrants receive government assistance. The standard of living for immigrants in the Netherlands, however, is higher than in most European nations.

## ▶ Education

The Dutch value education highly. Their government spends more than 5 percent of its budget—a fairly high percentage—on education. The country's literacy rate, or the percent of adults able to read and write a basic sentence, is 99 percent.

**Students at a primary school** in Arnhem, a city in the eastern Netherlands, raise their hands to answer a question.

Children may begin attending primary school at the age of four. Education becomes compulsory, or required by law, at the age of five. Primary instruction lasts eight years. English becomes part of the curriculum in the final year. Since schooling is required through the age of sixteen, all children advance to secondary schools. Schools are one of three types—general, pre-university, and vocational. Tests place pupils in the type of school that best fits their abilities and interests.

General secondary schools are classified as junior (offering a four-year course) or senior (five-year course). After six years of study, pre-university students may apply for entrance to an institution of higher education. Vocational schools offer many kinds of career preparation.

More than a dozen universities provide postsecondary education. William of Orange founded the oldest university, at Leiden, in 1575. The University of Groningen was established in 1614, and the University of Utrecht opened in 1636. The Dutch government funds all institutions of higher learning, whether public or private.

## ◉ Language

Dutch is the official language of the Netherlands. (Dutch is also an official language in the Caribbean countries of Aruba and the Netherlands Antilles.) Frisian is an official language in the northern province of Friesland. Both languages are of Germanic origin. Dutch people speak about twenty-five dialects, or variations, of Dutch. People in the Flanders region of Belgium speak a Dutch dialect called Flemish. New immigrants who don't speak Dutch must learn the language to get permits to stay in the country. Most school-children also learn English and German.

## Religion

Historically, most Dutch people have followed one of two branches of the Christian religion. Roman Catholicism still predominates in the south. About 30 percent of the population is Roman Catholic. Protestantism is more common in the north. About 20 percent of the population are members of a Protestant Christian church. The Protestant branch of Calvinism is the religion of 6 percent of the Dutch people, and 14 percent follow other Protestant faiths. Immigrants have brought the Islamic faith with them to the Netherlands, and almost 6 percent of the population is Muslim. The remaining 2 percent follow a variety of other religions, including Judaism. The largest percent of the population—about 42 percent—claims no religious affiliation.

The **Netherlands reports that 75 percent of its population speaks at least one other language besides Dutch. And 12 percent speak three or more foreign languages.**

The Netherlands has a long tradition of allowing freedom of religion. The Dutch have also kept religion separate from government. Religion has played a large role in shaping Dutch life and thought, however. The nation has produced many religious writers and thinkers. The Dutch often take a moral approach to human affairs. That is, even people who are not members of a church seriously consider the rightness or wrongness of political and social issues. The virtues of charity and honesty, for instance, remain key Dutch values.

Visit www.vgsbooks.com for links to websites to learn more about the people of the Netherlands and their language and religion.

# CULTURAL LIFE

The Dutch value creative expression so highly that 4 percent of their government's budget goes to support the arts. The Dutch are proud of their rich culture, and about one thousand museums showcase art in the Netherlands. Some of the most famous and influential painters in the history of world art were Dutch. The paintings of Rembrandt van Rijn, Johannes Vermeer, and Vincent van Gogh can be seen on everything from museum walls to cigar box labels. Modern Dutch artists express themselves freely in many media. The country also has a long tradition in music, dance, and other performing arts. Dutch writers and thinkers have excelled at scientific and religious writings, as well as fiction. The Dutch people have won eighteen Nobel Prizes, mostly in the field of physics and other sciences.

## ○ Visual Arts

The Netherlands is particularly strong in the visual arts. In about 1500, the fantastic and sometimes terrifying visions of Hieronymus

Bosch inspired his painting *The Garden of Earthly Delights*. A few years later, a movement called the Leiden School improved the technical aspects of painting and made realism popular. Worldly scenes—such as *The Chess Players* by Lucas van Leyden—gradually replaced religious themes as subjects in Dutch paintings.

During the Golden Age of the 1600s, wealthy merchants were the main patrons of Dutch art. They wanted artists to depict their middle-class lives. During this period, painter and printmaker Rembrandt van Rijn created hundreds of pieces of art. His ability to catch personality in a portrait is one reason Rembrandt is considered one of the world's greatest artists. This ability can be seen in his painting *The Dutch Masters*. Many people know it as a famous cigar box label, since 1911. Rembrandt also painted and sketched many portraits of himself over his lifetime.

Though Johannes Vermeer has only thirty-five paintings to his name, his work represents the Golden Age. With a subtle play of light

Visitors to the Rijksmuseum in Amsterdam look at Rembrandt van Rijn's famous painting **Night Watch.**

and texture, he added mystery and humanity to his scenes of Dutch middle-class life. The unknown model in *Girl with a Pearl Earring*, for instance, gazes out of the canvas as if she is about to speak.

Many other artists excelled during the Golden Age. Frans Hals, Rembrandt's contemporary, also achieved fame for portraiture. His richly colored canvases of everyday events convey realism and spontaneity. Artists such as Jacob van Ruisdael and Willem van de Velde accurately painted the Dutch landscape around them.

Nineteenth-century Dutch art reached its creative heights in the works of Vincent van Gogh. Thick oil paint and intense colors give strong feelings and a sense of movement to his paintings. His expressive style had an enormous influence on modern art, and art critics consider him one of the world's great painters. In his short and troubled life, however, he was largely unknown.

**Vincent van Gogh** often painted self-portraits. Few photographs of him are known to exist. This one dates to 1871.

In the twentieth century, M. C. Escher used math to create prints that puzzle the eye. A movement called De Stijl (the style) helped to revolutionize the world of art and architecture. This group of painters and architects favored clean lines and minimal decoration. Piet Mondrian is the most important of the De Stijl artists. He produced abstract paintings of lines and colors. Architects in the movement included Gerrit Rietveld and Willem Dudok. Modern Dutch architects have changed the appearance of urban buildings by using large glass windows to let in sunlight and by introducing brightly colored exteriors.

In the twenty-first century, some Dutch artists paint in the realistic style. Others explore the frontiers of digital and multimedia art. In 2007 artist Jeroen Henneman created the sculpture *De Schreeuw* (The Scream) as a symbol of free speech. It stands in a public park in Amsterdam. The 15-foot-high (4.5 m) stainless steel sculpture shows a face in profile, crying out. It is in memory of Theo van Gogh, the outspoken filmmaker who was murdered in 2004.

Adriaan Geuze and his West 8 design team create award-winning parks, squares, and gardens in urban areas. Named for the force-8 (storm strength) winds that blow off the North Sea, the group seeks to create harmony between nature and industry. West 8 was responsible for planting twenty-five thousand birch trees at Amsterdam's Schiphol Airport, for instance. The firm continues to design landscapes and open spaces for the airport and other public places.

# Literature

Some of the most noted Dutch writers have taken religion, philosophy, and law as their subjects. Beatrice of Nazareth (1200–1268) was the first known prose writer in the Dutch language. A Catholic nun, she wrote a book about spirituality called *Seven Ways of Holy Love.* Two centuries later, philosopher and Catholic priest Desiderius Erasmus stressed the importance of tolerance, kindness, devotion, and honesty. His way of thinking came to be called humanism. Erasmus wrote during the Protestant Reformation, when Europe was torn by religious differences between Catholics and Protestants. He sought reforms that would keep the Christian community together.

Baruch Spinoza (1632–1677) was a Dutch philosopher whose Jewish parents had fled from Portugal to escape religious persecution. Spinoza grew up as a freethinker—a person who is guided by rational thought, not religious

In a letter to a friend, Dutch writer and book lover Erasmus said, "When I get a little money I buy books; and if any is left I buy food and clothes."

doctrine. His broad-minded ideas helped lay the groundwork for the Enlightenment—a way of thinking that promoted science and reason.

Eduard Douwes Dekker was a colonial administrator in Southeast Asia in the 1800s. He wrote under the name Multatuli. His novel *Max Havelaar* (1860) savagely criticized the Dutch treatment of the local people in Dutch colonies. The book caused many Dutch to demand fairer treatment of colonial peoples. As a result of this public outcry, the national legislature began to reform its colonial policy.

During World War II, Anne Frank recorded her life in hiding with her Jewish family in Amsterdam. Frank died in a concentration camp shortly before the war's end. But her diary survived and was first published as *The Annex* in 1947. It was soon published in English as *Anne Frank: Diary of a Young Girl*. Marga Minco was a young Dutch Jewish woman who survived World War II. In 1957 she won success at home and abroad with her first novel *Het bittere kruid* (*Bitter Herbs*), based on her own experiences during the war.

Modern Dutch poets and novelists, including Jan Wolkers and G. K. van't Reve, often write about the challenges of living in a highly urban and industrial society. Cees Nooteboom tackles serious philosophical topics. His novels, poetry, and travel writing are widely respected and are translated into many languages. Harry Mulisch's best-selling novel *De ontdekking van de Hemel* (1992) was made into an English-language movie called *The Discovery of Heaven* in 2001. A story about angels that affect the lives of humans, it reflects the author's interest in history, philosophy, and religion. The plot suggests that everything happens for a reason.

*Left:* **Eduard Douwes Dekker** wrote in the 1800s under the name Multatuli, which means "I have suffered much." *Right:* **Harry Mulisch** is a best-selling modern Dutch author.

Dick Bruna is a well-known Dutch children's author and illustrator. His most famous character is a cute rabbit called Miffy. She looks somewhat like a Japanese "Hello Kitty" character, but she is much older. Miffy turned fifty in 2005.

In 2005 *Time* magazine named Dutch Somali writer, thinker, and politician Ayaan Hirsi Ali one of the one hundred most influential people in the world. A former Muslim, she strongly supports Western values, such as freedom of expression. Hirsi Ali speaks against the limitations she sees in Islamic culture. She wrote the script of Theo van Gogh's short film *Submission*, which criticized the treatment of women in Islam. Her 2007 autobiography is called *Infidel*.

> **The Dutch have a well-deserved reputation for being imaginative, orderly, and punctual (on time). Christian Huygens invented the pendulum clock in 1657. A hanging weight that swings back and forth runs the clock. In the same era, Anton van Leeuwenhoek perfected the microscope.**

## ▶ Film

Dutch films have won worldwide acclaim. Filmmaker Paul Verhoeven's love story *Turkish Delight* won an Academy Award for Best Foreign Language Film in 1974. Working in the United States, he directed popular hits such as *RoboCop*, *Basic Instinct*, and *Starship Troopers*. He returned to the Netherlands in 2006 to direct *Black Book*, which he also cowrote. It tells the story of a Dutch Jewish woman who becomes a spy for the underground resistance during World War II.

In 1996 film director Theo van Gogh won a Golden Calf, considered the Dutch Oscar, for *Blind Date*. In 2008 U.S. director Stanley Tucci remade the movie, which is about a couple trying to stay together after the death of their child.

Dutch animator Michael Dudok De Wit's short film *Father and Daughter* won the Academy Award for Best Animated Short Film in 2000. Only 8.5 minutes long, the lovely movie shows a girl growing up without her father, set against the landscape of the Netherlands.

## ▶ Music

Unlike the visual arts, Dutch music was not much developed in the Golden Age. In modern times, however, Dutch musicians excel at all musical forms, from classical music to hip-hop to jazz. The Amsterdam Royal Orchestra is especially well known and respected. The Netherlands Opera performs ten operas a year. Opera singer Charlotte Margiano excels at singing roles in operas by Mozart.

The North Sea Jazz Festival is well attended every summer. Dutch jazz singer Denise Jannah adds touches of Surinamese music from her homeland to her interpretation of U.S. jazz standards. The music genre called World Music flourishes in international Amsterdam. Especially popular is Latin music, from Cuban salsa to Argentine tango.

## Holidays

New Year's Day, on January 1, is a public holiday in the Netherlands. Carnival falls in February or March. For Christians, it marks the last day before Lent, the somber season leading up to Easter. In the Catholic south, people celebrate Carnival with rowdy parties. Easter weekend (Friday through Monday) is an official holiday. Sporting events take place on Easter Monday. Whit Monday, seven weeks after Easter, is also a public holiday.

Spring is a time of many celebrations. Queen's Day on April 30 marks the day Queen Beatrix became queen in 1980. It was also the birthday of her mother, Juliana. People celebrate with parades, fairs, and contests. During springtime flower festivals, the Dutch decorate floats with tulips and other blooms. Liberation Day on May 5 marks the end of the German occupation in 1945.

While schools and businesses don't close for it, the third Thursday in September is a public event in The Hague. On that day, the queen rides through the city in a golden coach, on her way to officially open a new session of parliament.

On December 5, people celebrate Saint Nicholas's Eve. The saint, or holy man, was supposed to protect sailors, and the port city of Amsterdam claimed Nicholas as its patron saint (protector). Saint Nicholas's name in Dutch—Sint Nicolass, or Sinter Claes—is the root of the name Santa Claus. In Amsterdam a person dressed as Saint Nicholas rides through the streets on this holiday. Bells, loud

### BROKEN CHAINS

On July 1, Amsterdam celebrates the holiday of Keti Koti, or Emancipation Day. It remembers the date in 1863 when the Dutch abolished slavery in their colonies. *Keti koti* means "broken chains" in Surinamese, the language of Suriname. Festivities include colorful dress, lively salsa and reggae music, and Caribbean foods. In modern times, Amsterdam is home to many people of Caribbean ancestry. In the past, the city saw fierce debates between merchants who made fortunes from the slave trade and abolitionists, who wanted to end slavery. At the end of the day, the mayor of Amsterdam lays a wreath at the National Monument of Slavery.

cannons, and cheering crowds greet his arrival. The Dutch exchange gifts on this day as well as on Christmas.

Dutch Muslims celebrate Islamic holidays. Their dates change every year, as Islam follows a lunar, or moon-based, calendar. The most important time in Islam is the month of Ramadan. It honors the time when the prophet (spiritual spokesperson) Muhammad received the words of the Quran, Islam's holy book. During this month, observant Muslims do not eat or drink anything from sunrise to sunset. The end of the month sees three days of celebration, called Eid al-Fitr.

## ● Sports and Recreation

Sports are very popular in the Netherlands. Besides playing sports for fun, many people compete through sports clubs. Soccer, called football outside of the United States, is the country's most popular sport. Among the country's largest sporting clubs is the Royal Netherlands Football Association, with millions of members. Track and field, baseball, swimming, sailing, ice hockey, and field hockey are also very popular. Sandy beaches along the North Sea attract locals and tourists, though the water is often cold. Tennis, volleyball, and badminton are favorite net sports. Almost every Dutch person owns a bicycle, and bike paths run through the country. People ride bikes in races as well as for transportation.

Some games are native to the Netherlands. *Korfbal* combines elements of soccer and basketball. In Friesland, some people play *kaatsen*. In this team sport, players use their hands to hit a small soft ball. The Friesland sport of *fierljeppen* involves vaulting over a wide ditch with the help of a long pole.

A vaulting competitor takes part in the Dutch Championship Fierljeppen.

Ice-skating is a national sport. In the 2010 Winter Olympics in Canada, Dutch speed skater Sven Kramer won a gold medal and set a record time in the 5,000-meter (3-mile) speed skating race. In winter many Dutch enjoy long-distance skating on the country's frozen canals. When winters are cold enough, Friesland hosts a daylong ice-skating race. Called the Elfstedentocht (Eleven Cities Tour), the route travels 125 miles (200 km) on the frozen lakes, rivers, and canals that connect eleven towns in Friesland. In most years, temperatures have not dropped low enough for this race to take place.

Visit www.vgsbooks.com for links to websites with additional information about cultural traditions in the Netherlands.

## Food

The Dutch usually eat three meals a day. Breakfast often consists of sliced Dutch cheese or meats and boiled eggs. Bread or toast is topped with jelly, chocolate spread, or chocolate sprinkles called *hagelslag*. Lunch may be a deep-fried sausage or an open-faced sandwich of dark bread topped with slices of cold meat, cheese, and vegetables.

Dutch families gather for a large evening meal at about six o'clock. Dinner may begin with soup; followed by a pork chop or piece of beef; boiled or mashed potatoes; and a vegetable such as endive, kale, or carrots. Thick with vegetables and chunks of bacon and sausage, Dutch pea soup is a meal in itself.

Seafood is a large part of the Dutch diet. Eels and herring are popular. Raw herring is considered a treat. Those who like it pick up the cleaned and headless fish by its tail and let it slide slowly down their throats.

Traditional Dutch recipes are known for their simple, flavorful ingredients, such as butter, with few spices. Immigrants and colonists from former Dutch colonies have introduced spicier dishes. Indonesian food has become part of the Dutch diet. The

A chef makes *poffertjes*, a small Dutch pancake. Poffertjes stands are common on city streets throughout the Netherlands from September to March.

# THICK-CUT FRIES WITH SATAY SAUCE

Invented in Belgium, parts of which were once part of the Netherlands, french fries are very popular in the Netherlands. Called *patat*, or *friets*, the thick-cut fries come with a variety of toppings. The Dutch love to eat their fries with satay sauce, a peanut sauce from Indonesia. Baking fries uses less oil than frying, so it's healthier, and the fries taste just as good.

**Ingredients:**

4 large baking potatoes

2 tbsp. vegetable oil

salt

1. Wash and cut potatoes into wedges. Place wedges on a cookie sheet.
2. Drizzle the oil over the potatoes. Use a spatula to turn wedges until all are lightly coated in oil.
3. Bake for 30 minutes in a 450°F oven, or until potatoes begin to brown.
4. Place on paper towels, and sprinkle lightly with salt.

**Satay Sauce Ingredients:**

¼ small onion, finely chopped

1 tsp. vegetable oil

½ cup chunky peanut butter

½ cup coconut milk (or water)

juice of 1 lime

1 tbsp. brown sugar

½ tsp. red pepper flakes

1. In a large saucepan over medium heat, fry the onion in oil until soft.
2. Add all the other ingredients, and mix well.
3. Simmer on low heat for 5 minutes, stirring occasionally. If the sauce gets too thick, add some warm water.
4. Place satay sauce in a bowl for dipping, or pour over fries.

Serves 4 to 6

Indonesian *rijsttafel*, which means "rice table," is a celebratory meal. It consists of rice, a spicy hot sauce, and dozens of dishes to share.

Popular snacks include french fries sold at street stalls and small shops all over the country. Mayonnaise is the most common topping, not ketchup. French fries with Indonesian peanut sauce is a good—and a very popular—example of Indo-Dutch fusion. Waffles with whipped cream or warm caramel sauce are another favorite. Licorice is a common candy, including a salty variety. The Dutch enjoy high-quality chocolate. It is made locally from imported cacao beans (the source of cocoa).

# THE ECONOMY

The Netherlands has one of the healthiest and wealthiest economies in the world. Its workforce is well educated. Unemployment and inflation (rising prices) are moderate. While few people work in agriculture, Dutch farmers use modern machines and techniques to produce abundant food. Farmers sell their surplus to other countries and to food-processing factories. Other major industries produce chemicals, refined petroleum, and electrical machinery. Because of its waterways and seacoast, the Netherlands also plays an important role as a European transportation hub.

The nation's income depends heavily on trade with other countries, especially other members of the European Union. The EU began in 1993. It removed trade barriers, such as taxes, between member nations. The members became a single trading block with more buying power than each had on its own. In 2002 the Netherlands began using the euro, the common currency of the EU. The Netherlands also works closely with Belgium and Luxembourg in economic matters.

Together, the three nations cooperate to improve and expand trade and investment opportunities.

The Netherlands's economic growth fell in 2008 because of a world financial crisis. Despite this decline, the Dutch still enjoy one of the world's highest levels of income.

## ▶ Services

Service workers provide assistance to people, government, and businesses rather than producing goods. They hold jobs in teaching, health care, banking, law enforcement, transportation, arts, and communication. Import and export sales of goods is a cornerstone of the Dutch economy. The tourist industry employs many service workers too.

The service sector is by far the largest part of the Dutch economy. The sector brings in 73 percent of the nation's gross domestic product (GDP, the amount of money a country earns in a year). Jobs in services employ 80 percent of the workforce.

**Customers make their selections at a cheese shop in Amsterdam.** The selling of cheese in the Netherlands illustrates the interlinking of agriculture, trade, tourism, and services.

## ◉ Trade

Trade has long been the lifeline of the Dutch economy. The EU nation of Germany is the Netherlands's leading trade partner. The Rhine River, a busy commercial route, links the two countries. The Dutch have also sold large supplies of natural gas to Germany. The unit of Belgium-Luxembourg ranks second to Germany as a Dutch trading partner, followed by France and Britain. Top exports (goods sold to other countries) are machinery and equipment, chemicals, fuels, and food—especially cheese and other dairy products. Top imports bought from other countries include machinery and transportation equipment, chemicals, fuels, food, and clothing. The country must also import most of the raw materials its industries need.

The Netherlands is one of the wealthiest nations in the world. It ranks third in the world for the amount of money per person donated to international aid and projects to help low-income countries develop their economies. The Dutch are especially committed to ending poverty in Africa.

Thirty percent of all goods shipped to or from Western European countries pass through Dutch seaports. Rotterdam's Europort expanded its facilities in the 1980s to include petrochemical, oil, and other manufacturing complexes. A deep channel dug in the North Sea allows the port to handle heavy tankers. Rotterdam is among the world's chief oil ports and markets. Oil is bought and sold there daily, and pipelines move the petroleum from Rotterdam to Germany and Belgium.

## ▶ Tourism

About 10 million people visit the Netherlands each year. The nation earns more than $7 billion annually from tourism. Travelers interested in history and culture are attracted by the country's one thousand museums. They include the Rijksmuseum in Amsterdam, the Mauritshuis in The Hague, and the Palace Het Loo in Apeldoorn.

Dutch towns and cities have distinctive characters. Amsterdam—with its canals, bridges, and seventeenth-century houses—is a dynamic, modern city. The Hague, the official residence of Queen Beatrix, contains many parks and shopping arcades. One of the districts of The Hague is the seaside resort of Scheveningen. Rotterdam is famous for its enormous port facilities and futuristic architecture.

Biking along the level roads of the Netherlands is a favorite outdoor activity for summer visitors. Most tourists arrive during the flower season from March to September. In those months, millions of tulips, daffodils, and hyacinths carpet South Holland.

Tourists and residents crowd the beach at Scheveningen. *Inset:* The Rijksmuseum in Amsterdam contains a large collection of paintings from the Dutch Golden Age.

## ▶ Industry

The industrial sector, including construction trades and mining, accounts for about 25 percent of the nation's GDP and employs 18 percent of the workforce. The Netherlands did not develop large-scale industries until about 1890, when coal mining, chemical manufacturing, and electrical business were established. Since then the country has become highly industrialized, primarily through the efforts of private companies. Foreign investment has helped finance the nation's economic growth since 1950. The United States, for instance, invests heavily in Dutch businesses.

The Netherlands's leading industrial products are chemicals, petroleum, metals, and processed foods. Dutch companies produce top-of-the-line high-technology products such as microcomputers and precision equipment. Shipbuilding, an age-old Dutch industry, has declined in importance. Hydraulic (water-related) engineering and construction is very important in the low-lying country.

Some of the world's biggest industries are based in the Netherlands. They include the electronics leader Philips and the petroleum company Royal Dutch Shell. The Dutch-British corporation Unilever owns many recognizable food brands, such as Kraft and Nestlé. PolyGram NV is a giant music company that owns Motown Records and other major labels.

### HIGH-TECH

When you listen to music or watch movies at home, you can partly thank the Philips Company of the Netherlands. It is one of the largest electronics companies in the world. Philips released the first home video recorder in 1963, the compact disk (CD) in 1982, the DVD in the mid-1990s, and Blu-ray technology in 2006. These are just a few of Philips's products. The company has registered about thirty-three thousand trademarks on original products and forty-nine thousand product designs.

## ▶ Mining and Energy

By the 1970s, natural gas in the Netherlands had replaced coal as an energy source. Oil deposits in the North Sea competed in volume with the gas finds. Dutch oil platforms dot the surface of this stormy arm of the Atlantic Ocean.

Access to natural gas and petroleum has made the Netherlands a major energy producer. Small reserves of natural gas in the north are being worked in order to conserve the larger deposits in the huge Groningen Field. The gas field is the largest on the European continent. Natural gas meets about 50 percent of the country's energy needs. Oil accounts for 37 percent. Royal

Dutch Shell operates oil platforms in the North Sea. Most crude oil is imported, however, and is then refined and exported. Imported coal supplies 13 percent, and the Netherlands's two nuclear power plants supply about 1 percent of the nation's energy.

Natural gas supplies are dwindling, causing the loss of an important source of revenue. The Netherlands will have to find new energy sources, and they will likely be costly. The country has installed more than two thousand wind turbines.

## Agriculture

About 2 percent of the Dutch are engaged in agriculture, including farming, fishing, and forestry. The sector brings in 2 percent of the nation's GDP. The country is one of the largest exporters of food in the world. Most of the more than eighty thousand farms in the Netherlands are small, family-owned operations. The government encourages farmers to combine their holdings into larger estates to increase agricultural efficiency.

About 65 percent of the country's land is used for agriculture. More than 60 percent of this farmland is pasture for animals. Crops grow on 32 percent of agricultural land, and 6 percent supports horticulture (the growing of fruits and flowers). The Netherlands produces enough flowers and dairy products to export.

### BILLIONS OF BLOOMS

Flowers are big business in the Netherlands. Flower farms cover 88 square miles (228 sq. km) of land—enough to cover more than thirty thousand football fields. The farms produce more than 8 billion flowers. But the Netherlands doesn't just grow and sell its own flowers. Dutch florist companies also import and export flowers from Africa. Every year growers in Kenya and other African countries ship about 1.7 billion roses by air to Dutch wholesalers. They sell most of the flowers to other European Union countries.

A farmer in North Holland works in a tulip bulb field.

The country's five million dairy cattle are the basis of a large milk-processing industry. Breeds of Dutch dairy cattle, particularly Holsteins, are high-yielding milkers. Dutch cheese—notably Edam and Gouda—and other Dutch milk products are sold throughout the world.

Dutch farmers also raise nearly 14 million pigs and 7 million sheep. The Netherlands imports large quantities of grain to feed its livestock. Pork, mutton, and poultry are shipped to EU partners and to other parts of the world. Dutch environmentalists are concerned about sewage and other wastes from pigs and cattle that pollute groundwater supplies.

The most significant outdoor crops are potatoes, sugar beets, and wheat. Farmers plant corn as fodder (food for livestock). Small farms produce fresh fruits and vegetables for local consumption and for export. Major fruits and vegetables are tomatoes, apples, cucumbers, carrots, mushrooms, and pears. Farmers grow some foods in greenhouses. To make their businesses profitable, greenhouse owners use energy-saving measures on a large scale.

More than half of the world's exported flowers come from the Netherlands. Flowers and bulbs are among the most important Dutch agricultural exports. The flower industry consists of thousands of small, family-owned businesses. Individual Dutch growers often specialize in one type of plant. For instance, tulip producers do not cultivate any other type of flower. Farmers obtain seeds from specialists who work to improve plant varieties. Teams of scientists at testing stations provide vital support by sharing new knowledge with growers. Besides tulips, the Dutch also raise lilies, daffodils, gladioli, and hyacinths. Merchants at the Aalsmeer auction near Amsterdam sell millions of cut flowers and potted plants every day.

**A farmer tends tomato plants in his greenhouse.** The Netherlands is the number one exporter of greenhouse products in Europe.

A commercial Dutch fishing trawler heads home after a fishing expedition.

# Fishing

More than nine hundred Dutch fishing vessels ply the Atlantic. Fishing is not as important to the Dutch economy as it once was. Since the 1970s, overfishing in the North Sea has caused a rapid decline in the population of herring—the principal Dutch catch for many centuries. The Netherlands's few remaining herring trawlers sail as far as Iceland in search of this popular fish. Mackerel and plaice are other popular catches. Fishing boats travel southward for plaice and sole. Other vessels bring in shrimp and crab off the Dutch coast.

# Transportation

The Netherlands has a well-developed transportation network of railways, roads, and water routes. Of the country's 84,177 miles (135,470 km) of roads, about half are highways. Several superhighways connect to Germany's extensive road system. The country has 1,747 miles (2,811 km) of railways. Most trains run on electricity.

The Netherlands has one of Europe's best public transportation systems. Trains connect many cities. Buses and trams (streetcars) serve urban areas, and Amsterdam and Rotterdam also have subways.

## NOT SO SMART

In overcrowded cities, some Dutch drive Smart ForTwos: fuel-efficient German microcars that seat two people. Amsterdam police are concerned about Smart *smijten*, or Smart tipping: cases of drunken vandals pushing the little cars into canals. People who back their cars into parking spaces along the water's edge may find that someone has lifted its front end and hoisted the Smart car into the canal. A night under water usually ruins a car forever.

## THE FLYING DUTCH

KLM (Royal Dutch Airlines) is the world's longest-flying airline. It has been in business since 1919, when Queen Wilhelmina gave it its "royal" designation. From 1929 until 1939, KLM's service between Amsterdam and Indonesia was the world's longest-distance regular, scheduled flight.

One-third of Dutch commercial traffic moves on the country's inland waterways. The system is longer than its rail network. The rivers of the Netherlands also carry goods from Amsterdam and Rotterdam—the country's main ports—to other parts of Europe. Dutch ports together rank third in the world in the amount of cargo they handle, much of it involving the importing and exporting of natural gas and petroleum.

Another connection to Europe and the world is through the national airline, Royal Dutch Airlines (KLM). There are twenty airports with paved runways in the Netherlands. The major airport is Schiphol, outside of Amsterdam.

## Drugs and Crime

The crime rate in the Netherlands is low compared to crime rates in the United States and many European countries. Marijuana use is legal only in coffee shops that have special licenses to sell it. Use among young Dutch people of hard drugs such as cocaine and heroin is low. But the country is also an important gateway for illegal hard drugs entering Europe. And it is a major maker of illegal drugs for export,

**Royal Dutch Airlines (KLM)** is the oldest airline in the world flying under its original name. The airline's hub is Schiphol Airport in Amsterdam.

especially ecstasy. People also use the nation's large banking and financial sector to launder, or transmit, money from illegal businesses such as drug trafficking.

## Media and Communications

Freedom of the press is guaranteed by the Dutch constitution, as is free speech. Public radio and TV channels face stiff competition from commercial stations. The TV market is very competitive. Viewers have access to a wide range of domestic and foreign channels, thanks to high rates of cable and satellite TV use. Every province has at least one local public TV channel. The three national public TV stations enjoy high audience shares.

The Dutch enjoy a highly developed and well-maintained communications network. The country has more cell phones (17 million) than people (16.5 million) and 15 million Internet users. Only 7 million landlines are installed.

Visit www.vgsbooks.com for links to websites with up-to-the minute news in the Netherlands as well as more information about the economic climate in the Netherlands.

## The Future

The Dutch are generally hopeful about the future. Historically, they have worked hard to tackle tough goals. They have won many victories, such as turning back the sea and providing benefits for all the nation's citizens. Modern challenges include integrating immigrants into Dutch society and fighting the global economic downturn that began in 2008. The nation is well prepared to face its difficulties. It can rely on a healthy and well-educated workforce and a modern financial and communications network. As a member of the European Union with ample natural resources, the Netherlands is likely to continue to prosper.

**CA. 3000 B.C.**  Burial mounds made out of huge stones show evidence of an early culture in the area of the Netherlands.

**15 B.C.**  The Roman Empire takes over the lands of the Belgae, in the present-day southern Netherlands and northern Belgium.

**LATE A.D. 600s**  The Franks gain control of most of the Netherlands.

**814**  Charlemagne, leader of the Frankish Empire, dies. During the next one hundred years, the Netherlands passes into the hands of several different rulers.

**925**  The East Frankish Kingdom (modern Germany) wins control of the Netherlands.

**1419**  Philip, Duke of Burgundy (in modern France), begins to expand his holdings. Rich merchants in the northern lowlands welcome his rule.

**1482**  Citizens of Amsterdam wall in their coastal town to protect it from attacks and floods.

**1512**  Erasmus publishes his *Praise of Folly*. By using humor to pretend to praise foolishness, Erasmus calls attention to the need for serious church reforms.

**1519**  Emperor Charles V of Spain inherits the Burgundian lands.

**1555**  Philip II, the son of Charles V, becomes the ruler of both Spain and the Netherlands. His government oppresses Dutch Protestant Christians and taxes the populace heavily.

**1568**  William I of Orange leads a Dutch rebellion against Philip II's Spanish rule, beginning the Dutch War of Independence (1568-1648).

**1575**  William of Orange founds the country's first university, at Leiden.

**1581**  The Dutch United Provinces declare their independence from Spain. This marks the beginning of the Netherlands as a separate political unit.

**1600s**  During this century, called the Golden Age, the Netherlands is a leading force in European business and art.

**1602**  Merchants form the Dutch East India Company to trade directly with Asian countries.

**1621**  The Dutch West India Company starts a colony in North America called New Netherland—later to be New York.

**1648**  The Dutch War of Independence ends. Spain recognizes the Netherlands's independence and gives the Dutch the Caribbean islands of the Netherlands Antilles and Aruba.

**1795**  France occupies the Netherlands.

1815    European forces defeat Napoleon. The Dutch form the Kingdom of the Netherlands. William becomes the first Dutch king, King William I.

1819    The Netherlands abolishes the Atlantic slave trade—but not slavery.

1839    Belgium declares independence from the Kingdom of the Netherlands.

1863    The Netherlands abolishes slavery in Dutch colonies.

1890    Luxembourg ends its union with the Netherlands and becomes an independent state.

1919    The Netherlands grants voting rights to women in 1919.

1932    A 19-mile (30 km) dam that blocks the Zuiderzee forms the shallow Waddenzee and the freshwater Lake IJssel.

1940    Germany occupies the Netherlands in May, during World War II (1939-1945).

1947    Titled *The Annex*, the first edition of Anne Frank's wartime diary is published.

1949    The Netherlands joins the North Atlantic Treaty Organization (NATO). After four years of fighting, Indonesia wins its independence from the Dutch.

1953    North Sea flooding kills 1,850 people and destroys property. Dutch engineers plan the Delta Project to build a system of dams in response.

1959    Scientists find large natural gas deposits in the Netherlands.

1975    Suriname becomes independent. Thousands of Surinamese move to the Netherlands.

1980    Queen Juliana steps down, and her daughter Beatrix becomes queen.

1993    The European Union is founded. The Netherlands is one of the founding members.

2000    The Netherlands legalizes euthanasia and same-sex marriage. Michael Dudok De Wit's short film *Father and Daughter* wins an Academy Award.

2002    The Dutch adopt the euro. In May an animal-rights activist murders politician Pim Fortuyn.

2004    A Dutch Moroccan man murders filmmaker Theo van Gogh.

2005    Parliament rules that new immigrants must pass a test in Dutch language and culture. The Dutch send troops to Afghanistan.

2008    A worldwide financial crisis causes the Dutch economy to decline.

2009    A man kills seven people and himself when he drives into a crowd in Apeldoorn.

2010    Dutch skater Sven Kramer wins a gold medal at the Winter Olympics. Prime Minister Balkenende resigns over disagreements about withdrawing Dutch troops from Afghanistan.

**COUNTRY NAME** Kingdom of the Netherlands

**AREA** 16,036 square miles (41,532 sq. km)

**MAIN LANDFORMS** High Netherlands, Low Netherlands, West Frisian Islands

**HIGHEST POINT** Vaalser Mountain, 1,053 feet (321 m) above sea level

**LOWEST POINT** Zuidplaspolder, 22 feet (7 m) below sea level

**MAJOR RIVERS** Meuse, Rhine, and Schelde

**ANIMALS** badgers, boars, deer, dormouse, foxes, pine martens, seals, midwife toad, wall lizard, coots, ducks, geese, herons, spoonbills, storks, swans, carp, eel, herring, mackerel, perch, pike, plaice

**CAPITAL CITY** Amsterdam (official); The Hague (seat of government)

**OTHER MAJOR CITIES** Rotterdam, Utrecht

**OFFICIAL LANGUAGES** Dutch and Frisian (in Friesland)

**MONETARY UNITY** Euro. 100 cents = 1 euro

## DUTCH CURRENCY

The Netherlands began using the euro in 2002. It is the common currency of the European Union. Euro banknotes, or paper money, come in seven different colors and denominations: 5, 10, 20, 50, 100, 200, and 500 euros. The eight coins are worth 1 and 2 euro, and then 1, 2, 5, 10, 20, and 50 cents. Each EU country that uses the euro provides its own national design for one side of the coin and uses a shared design on the other.

The Dutch coins bear one of two pictures of Queen Beatrix. Twelve stars that symbolize the EU surround her image.

The Netherlands's flag has three colored bands of equal size, running horizontally. From top to bottom, they are red, white, and blue. These are the colors of William of Orange, who led the Dutch revolt against Spanish rule in the late 1500s. The top band was originally orange, but because the color was prone to fading, it was eventually replaced with red.

"William of Nassau" is the national anthem of the Netherlands. Known as "The William," the song's title refers to William of Orange, the leader of the Dutch revolt against Philip II of Spain. It officially became the anthem in 1932 but has been in use since the 1600s, making it one of the oldest anthems in the world. Historians debate who wrote the words. One possibility is Philip Marnix van St. Aldegonde. The melody is based on an old tune from the 1500s.

The first and sixth verses of the song's fifteen verses make up the anthem.

| ENGLISH LYRICS | DUTCH LYRICS |
|---|---|
| William of Nassau, scion | Wilhelmus van Nassouwe |
| Of an old Germanic line, | Ben ik van Duitsen bloed |
| Dedicate undying | Den vaderland getrouwe |
| Faith to this land of mine. | Blijf ik tot in den dood |
| A prince I am, undaunted, | Een Prince van Oranjen |
| Of Orange, ever free, | Ben ik vrij onverveerd |
| To the king of Spain I've granted | Den Koning van Hispanjen |
| A lifelong loyalty. | Heb ik altijd geeerd |
| | |
| A shield and my reliance, | Mijn schild ende betrouwen |
| O God, Thou ever wert. | Zijt gij o God mijn Heer |
| I'll trust unto Thy guidance. | Op u zo wil ik bouwen |
| O leave me not ungirt. | Verlaat mij nimmermeer |
| That I may stay a pious | Dat ik doch vroom mag blijven |
| Servant of Thine for aye | Uw dienaar t'aller stond |
| And drive the plagues that try us | Die tirannie verdrijven |
| And tyranny away. | Die mij mijn hert doorwondt |

For a link to a site where you can listen to the Netherlands's national anthem, "William of Nassau," visit www.vgsbooks.com.

**BEATRIX WILHELMINA ARMGARD** (b. 1938) Born in Baarn, Beatrix became queen and chief of state in 1980, when her mother Juliana stepped down. As a child during World War II, Beatrix was sent to Canada for safety. She studied law at Leiden University. Her professional and caring yet low-key approach to being queen has made her popular. She is also committed to a number of social causes. Beatrix's son Willem-Alexander (b. 1967) is the heir apparent, or the person who will become the next monarch. If and when he becomes King William IV, he will be the Netherlands's first male monarch since 1890.

**DESIDERIUS ERASMUS** (1466–1536) Born in Rotterdam, Erasmus was a scholar and a Catholic priest. His writing was important in the rise of humanism: a way of thinking that stresses the importance of individual humans and their ability to use reason, not supernatural belief, to improve themselves. His most famous work is *The Praise of Folly* (1512). By using humor to pretend to praise foolishness, Erasmus called attention to the need for serious church reforms. Though Erasmus stayed loyal to the Catholic Church, his work helped spark the Protestant Reformation.

**ANNE FRANK** (1929–1945) Frank was born into a Jewish family in Frankfurt, Germany. Her family moved to Amsterdam in 1933 to escape growing anti-Semitism. During World War II, Nazi Germany occupied the Netherlands and persecuted Jews. In 1942 the Frank family secretly moved into the back annex of a building. Starting soon after her thirteenth birthday, Frank began recording her experiences of life in hiding in a diary. She wrote in Dutch. The family was arrested in 1944. Frank and her sister died of typhus and starvation in the Bergen-Belsen concentration camp in Germany shortly before the end of the war. After the war, her father found and published her diary. *Anne Frank: The Diary of a Young Girl* became a voice for the 1.5 million children the Nazis destroyed.

**AYAAN HIRSI ALI** (b.1969) Born in Mogadishu, Somalia, Hirsi Ali came to the Netherlands in 1992 and became a citizen in 1997. She is a Dutch feminist, activist, writer, and politician. A former Muslim, she supports Western-style freedoms and is an outspoken critic of Islam, which she considers antidemocratic. She wrote the screenplay for Theo van Gogh's 2004 movie *Submission*, criticizing the treatment of women in Islam. After a Muslim extremist murdered van Gogh in 2004, Hirsi Ali lived under police protection. The next year, *Time* magazine named her one of the most influential thinkers of modern times. Since 2007 she has lived in the United States.

**DENISE JANNAH** (b. 1956) Jannah is a Dutch jazz singer. She was born in Paramaribo, the capital of Suriname, South America, when the country was still part of the Kingdom of the Netherlands. She and her family moved to the Netherlands in the mid-1970s. Jannah studied law at the University of Utrecht before deciding to pursue her love of music. Music critics compare her rich, honey-toned voice to the voices of great jazz singers of the past, such as Ella Fitzgerald. Jannah has won the Edison Award twice, which is the Dutch equivalent of a Grammy Award.

**SVEN KRAMER** (b. 1986) Born in Heerenveen, Kramer is an Olympic champion speed ice-skater. In the 2010 Winter Olympic Games in Vancouver, Canada, he set an Olympic record when he skated the 5,000 meter (3-mile) race in 6 minutes 14.60 seconds. This is an average speed of almost 30 miles (48 km) per hour. His brother Brecht and his father, Yap, are also speed skaters.

**NAOMI VAN AS** (b. 1983) Born in The Hague, van As is a top-ranked field hockey player. She has been a member of the Dutch national team since 2003. She and the Dutch team beat China 2–0 to win the gold medal at the 2008 Summer Olympics in Beijing, China. Van As scored one of the Netherlands's two goals.

**THEO VAN GOGH** (1957–2004) Born in The Hague, van Gogh was a writer and a filmmaker. His great-grandfather, also named Theo, was the brother of the artist Vincent van Gogh. Theo Van Gogh supported freedom of speech. His strongly worded opinions against religion and other sensitive subjects offended a wide range of people. He received death threats after Dutch TV aired his ten-minute 2004 film *Submission*. The film showed words of the Quran on seminude women to criticize violence against women in Islam. A Dutch Muslim extremist murdered van Gogh. His death sparked an ongoing debate about the role of Muslim immigrants in Dutch society.

**REMBRANDT VAN RIJN** (1606–1669) Art historians consider Rembrandt the greatest painter of the Dutch Golden Age. Born in Leiden, Rembrandt was the son of a miller. He lived and worked in Amsterdam, and visitors can tour his house. Rembrandt's portrait paintings were famous in the Netherlands and abroad during his lifetime for the way they captured an individual's character. One of his best-known paintings is the *Night Watch*. His ability to capture light on canvas is obvious in this picture of a group of musketeers stepping out of dark shade into bright sunlight. It hangs in the Rijksmuseum in Amsterdam.

**PAUL VERHOEVEN** (b. 1938) Verhoeven is a Dutch filmmaker. Born in Amsterdam, he remembers living through bombing raids during World War II. In 1974 his love story *Turkish Delight* won an Academy Award for Best Foreign Language Film. Working in the United States, he directed popular hits such as *RoboCop*, *Basic Instinct*, and *Starship Troopers*. He returned to the Netherlands in 2006 to direct *Black Book*. It tells the story of a Dutch Jewish woman spy during World War II.

**AMSTERDAM** The Dutch capital is a beautiful playground. You can pedal or walk along canals, lined with narrow, historic buildings. Or rent pedal boats called canal bikes and pedal in the canals, along with the swans. Visit the Woonbootmuseum to see what it's like inside a houseboat. It's a powerful experience to enter the small rooms where Anne Frank and her family hid from the Nazis. World-class museums include the Rijkmuseum, which displays treasures from the Golden Age, including a famous collection of dolls' houses. Adults may enjoy the city's vibrant nightlife.

**DELFT** This delightful town is famous for its blue and white pottery. Visit on Thursdays to enjoy the market day in the central square. Delft was the home of the painter Vermeer in the seventeenth century, and the Museum Lambert van Meerten has a room decorated so you feel as if you've stepped into one of his paintings. You can climb the huge stone tower of the five-hundred-year-old Nieuwe Kerk (New Church) to get a bird's-eye view of the city.

**THE HAGUE** You can see the Netherlands's parliament buildings and the Peace Palace here, but you can also see them in miniature at the city's Madurodam. This is an amazing, highly detailed, pint-sized Dutch city. It incorporates real landmarks from around the country: castles, churches, and town halls; boats on canals, moving planes in airports, and windmills on farms. Afterward, have fun at Duinrell, a large amusement and water park.

**NETHERLANDS OPEN AIR MUSEUM** See what life was like for Dutch people in the 1800s at this open-air museum in Arnhem. Walk or take a tram around the park and through gardens. Witness the workings of a windmill and raising bridges. Historical workshops offer demonstrations of cheese making, shipbuilding, and paper making.

**ROTTERDAM** Rotterdam rebuilt with innovative new architecture after World War II. Nicknamed the Swan, the city's Erasmus Bridge soars over the largest harbor in Europe. Visitors enjoy the view from the space tower at the top of the 610-foot-tall (186 m) Euromast.

**WEERRIBBEN NATIONAL PARK** Migrating birds and nature lovers flock to the wetlands of this national park. Guides offer biking and boating trips, as well as special outings for children. A Nature Activities Center offers information and changing exhibits.

**WEST FRISIAN ISLANDS** A ferryboat ride takes visitors to this string of islands off North Holland, known for their beautiful forest and ocean landscape. Great sandy beaches are wonderful for swimming. Texel Island is the largest of the islands, where people can bike, hike, ride horses—or even try parachute jumping.

**anti-Semitism:** discrimination against Jews

**colony:** a territory ruled and occupied by a foreign power

**dike:** a levee or wall that serves to prevent flooding; from the Dutch word *dijk*

**Dutch East Indies:** Located in Southeast Asia, the Netherlands's largest and most important colony, beginning in 1602. The colony won independence in 1949 after a four-year war and formed the nation of Indonesia.

**European Union (EU):** a group of nations in Europe that agreed in 1993 to unite their markets so that people, trade goods, services, and money could move freely across borders. The union's goal is to strengthen the European economy and to reduce tensions among nations. By 2010 twenty-seven nations had become EU members. Sixteen of these, including the Netherlands, share a common currency called the euro.

**global warming:** the gradual increase in the average worldwide temperature of Earth's atmosphere

**gross domestic product (GDP):** the value of the goods and services produced by a country over a period of time, usually one year

**infant mortality rate (IMR):** the number of babies per 1,000 live births who die each year before their first birthday. The IMR is a key indicator of a country's social well-being.

**literacy:** the ability to read and write a basic sentence

**parliament:** a legislature, or group of lawmakers. The name comes from the French word *parler*, which means "to speak." Each member of parliament is called a minister. The prime minister, who serves as the country's head of government, is usually the leader of the party in power.

**polder:** an area of land that was once underwater. The Dutch create polders by building dikes around the area and pumping off the water.

**Quran:** the holy book of Islam. The prophet Muhammad dictated the book starting in A.D. 610. Muslims believe these scriptures come from God.

**satay sauce:** a peanut sauce, originally from Indonesia but often eaten with french fries in the Netherlands

**Bedrord, Neal, and Simon Sellars.** *The Netherlands.* **Footscray, Australia: Lonely Planet, 2007.**
Colorful and lively, this travel guide gives an overview of Dutch culture and history, as well as the usual maps and advice for travelers. You can find online information from the same publisher at www.lonelyplanet.com/the-netherlands.

**British Broadcasting Corporation.** *BBC News.* **2010.**
http://news.bbc.co.uk/ (January 2010).
This website is an extensive international news source. It contains regularly updated political and cultural news. The BBC's country profile of the Netherlands is at http://news.bbc.co.uk/2/hi/europe/country _profiles/1043423.stm.

**Central Intelligence Agency. "The World Factbook—Netherlands."** *The World Factbook.* **2009.**
https://www.cia.gov/library/publications/the-world-factbook/geos/countrytem-plate_nl.html (October 2009).
The U.S. CIA provides this general profile of the Netherlands. The profile includes brief summaries of the nation's geography, people, government, economy, communications, transportation, and military.

*CultureGrams: Europe.* **Vol. 2. Provo, UT: ProQuest, 2007.**
This volume reports on twenty-five cultural factors for European countries, including the Netherlands. It gives brief outlines of the Dutch language, general attitudes, the diet, the arts, and more.

*The Europa World Year Book, 2009.* **London: Routledge, 2009.**
This annual publication provides accurate, detailed information on the Netherlands and other countries of the world. It covers the country's recent history, economic affairs, government, education, statistics on health and welfare, and more.

**Janin, Hunt, and Ria Van Eil.** *Culture Shock! A Survival Guide to Customs and Etiquette: Netherlands.* **Tarrytwon, NY: Marshall Cavendish, 2008.**
Written for people who are going to live in the Netherlands, this book is an amusing read. It contains insights into local culture and traditions and advice on language and travel in the Netherlands. The authors explain common Dutch attitudes, such as the people's blunt honesty, as well as explaining features of the land, such as the engineering behind windmills and dikes.

**"PRB Data Finder: Netherlands." Population Reference Bureau (PRB). 2009.**
http://www.prb.org/Datafinder (October 2009).
The PRB provides a wealth of population, demographic, and health statistics for the Netherlands and almost all countries in the world.

*The Statesman's Yearbook: The Politics, Cultures and Economies of the World, 2010.* **Barry Turner, ed. New York: Macmillan, 2009.**
This annual publication provides concise information on the Netherlands, including its history, climate, government, economy, and culture, and relevant statistics.

**Thompson, Wayne C. *Western Europe, 2009*. Harpers Ferry, WV: Stryker-Post, 2009.**
Part of the World Today series, this book offers an in-depth article on the Netherlands. Maps, diagrams, and photographs accompany statistics and analysis of the Dutch economy, history, land, and culture.

**Travel for Kids: Netherlands. 2010.**
http://www.travelforkids.com/Funtodo/Netherlands/netherlands.htm (January 2010).
This kid-centered site supplies travel tips, photos, directions, book recommendations, and lots of ideas for fun adventures young people might enjoy all over the Netherlands.

**U.S. Department of State. "Background Notes: Netherlands." U.S. Department of State. 2009.**
http://www.state.gov/r/pa/ei/bgn/3204.htm (October 2009).
This website provides a general profile of the Netherlands, from the U.S. Department of State. The profile includes brief summaries of the nation's geography, people, government and politics, and economy.

**West 8 Urban Design and Landscape Architecture. 2010.**
http://www.west8.nl (February 2010).
The site of West 8 displays photographs of the company's landscape design of Amsterdam's Schiphol Airport, as well as many other design works in the Netherlands and around the world. Dutchman Adriaan Geuze founded the company in 1987.

**Chevalier, Tracy. *Girl with a Pearl Earring*. New York: HarperCollins, 1999.**
This best-selling novel imagines the life of Dutch painter Johannes Vermeer as he paints his famous picture *Girl with a Pearl Earring*. This tale of art, life, and passion during the seventeenth-century Golden Age in Vermeer's city of Delft was made into a major Hollywood film in 2003.

**Condon, Sean. *My 'Dam Life: Three Years in Holland*. Footscray, Australia: Lonely Planet, 2003.**
The Australian author is a comic writer who lived for three years in Amsterdam with his wife. He writes about everyday Dutch life, with a sharp eye for the absurd.

**De Bie, Ceciel, and Martijn Leenen. *Rembrandt*. Los Angeles: Getty Publications, 2001.**
This wonderfully illustrated book for younger readers explores the details of Rembrandt's paintings, including his major works such as *The Night Watch*. Also included are all Rembrandt's portraits of himself, from his youth to his old age.

**De Moor, Janny. *Dutch Cooking: Traditions, Ingredients, Tastes and Techniques*. Dallas: Aquamarine, 2008.**
This nicely illustrated book presents more than eighty traditional Dutch recipes.

**Discover the Netherlands**
http://www.discoverthenetherlands.org
Every other month, this site for kids offers a short film about something typically Dutch. It also answers FAQs (frequently asked questions) and lists fun facts, information about famous people, and more.

**Expatica: Netherlands**
http://www.expatica.com/nl/main.html
This English-language site for non-Dutch people living in the Netherlands is updated daily. The site includes news articles, tips on life in the Netherlands, information for students, and more.

**Frank, Anne. *Anne Frank: Diary of a Young Girl*. Phoenix: Heritage Publishers, 2009.**
Since it was first published in its original Dutch in 1947, this diary has become one of the most powerful voices of the Holocaust (a mass slaughter of Europeans, especially Jews, by the Nazis during World War II). Frank's record of courage, understanding, and hope in the face of hardship has been translated into dozens of languages. It is one of the most widely read books in the world.

**Raczka, Bob. *The Vermeer Interviews*. Minneapolis: Millbrook Press, 2009.**
In this look at seven paintings by Dutch artist Jan Vermeer, author Bob Raczka takes on the role of interviewer and the people in the paintings become his willing subjects. From *The Milkmaid* to *The Geographer*, Raczka teases out fascinating details about these gorgeous works of art and their mysterious creator.

**Schama, Simon.** *The Embarrassment of Riches: An Interpretation of Dutch Culture in the Golden Age.* **New York: Knopf, 1987.**
This fascinating book looks at the social history of the Golden Age, from patriotism to children's lives. Schama says, "The most extraordinary invention of this country . . . was its own culture." He shows how Dutch culture arose out of a group of people who in the early 1500s did not share a common nation, religion, or language. Quotes and illustrations enliven the text.

**Seward, Pat, and Sunandini Arora.** *The Netherlands.* **New York: Benchmark Books, 2006.**
Part of the Cultures of the World series, this book for younger readers offers an introduction to the geography, history, government, economy, people, and culture of the Netherlands.

**Van Oostrom, Frits, ed.** *The Netherlands in a Nutshell: Highlights from Dutch History and Culture.* **Amsterdam: Amsterdam University Press, 2008.**
This collection is a mine of information about the highlights of Dutch history. The authors are specialists, but members of the Dutch general public chose the topics.

*vgsbooks.com*
**http://www.vgsbooks.com**
Visit vgsbooks.com, the home page of the Visual Geography Series®. You can get linked to all sorts of useful online information, including geographical, historical, demographic, cultural, and economic websites. The vgsbooks.com site is a great resource for late-breaking news and statistics about countries around the world, including the Netherlands.

**Wolf, Manfred, ed.** *Amsterdam: A Traveler's Literary Companion.* **Berkeley, CA: Whereabouts Press, 2001.**
This is a collection of twenty stories by authors from Amsterdam, including Harry Mulisch, Cees Nooteboom, and Marga Minco. They present a side of Amsterdam tourists may never see. Many of the stories appear in this book in English for the first time.

**Captions for photos appearing on cover and chapter openers:**

Cover: The sun sets behind the Keizersgracht in Amsterdam, Netherlands. The Keizersgracht, or Emperor's Canal, is the widest of the four main canals in Amsterdam—the nation's capital city.

pp. 4–5 The Albert Cuyp Market in Amsterdam is one of the largest daily markets in Europe, attracting both residents and tourists.

pp. 8–9 Tulips are a popular and money-earning crop in the Netherlands. Windmills, originally built to pump water out of low-lying areas, dot the landscape throughout the Netherlands.

pp. 18–19 These huge stones are tombs called Hunebed, or dolmen, which date from the 3000s B.C. These Hunebed are in Drenthe in the northeastern part of the Netherlands.

pp. 38–39 Dutch people and tourists in the Netherlands ride bicycles both for transportation and recreation.

pp. 46–47 Citizens of Amsterdam hit the streets and canals to celebrate Queen's Day, a national celebration of the day Queen Beatrix became queen in 1980, which is celebrated on April 30. People often wear orange on this day because the queen is the princess of the House of Orange-Nassau.

pp. 56–57 An oil tanker docks in an industrial area of Rotterdam. The port city of Rotterdam is one of the largest trading centers in the Netherlands and Europe.

## Photo Acknowledgments

The images in this book are used with the permission of: © Jochem Wijnands/Lineair/Photolibrary, pp. 4–5; © XNR Productions, pp. 6, 10; © Eric Gevaert/Dreamstime.com, pp. 8–9; © age fotostock/SuperStock, pp. 12, 16; © Europe-Holland/Alamy, p. 14 (top); © Paul Oomen/Photographer's Choice/Getty Images, p. 14 (bottom); © Buiten-Beeld/Alamy, p. 14 (bottom inset); © Albert Knapp/Alamy, pp. 18–19; © The Bridgeman Art Library/Getty Images, pp. 20, 28; © Rochdale Art Gallery, Lancashire, UK/The Bridgeman Art Library, p. 21; The Art Archive/University Library Geneva/Gianni Dagli Orti, pp. 23, 25; The Art Archive/Château de Rambouillet/Gianni Dagli Orti, p. 26; Musee de la Dynastie, Brussels, Belgium/Patrick Lorette Giraudon/The Bridgeman Art Library, p. 30; © Hulton Archive/Getty Images, p. 31; © Hugo Jaeger/Timepix/Time & Life Pictures/Getty Images, p. 32; AP Photo, p. 34; AP Photo/Remy de la Mauviniere, p. 35 (left); © LEX VAN LIESHOUT/AFP/Getty Images, pp. 35 (right), 62; © Profimedia International s.r.o./Alamy, pp. 38–39; © Picture Contact/Alamy, p. 40; © Frans Lemmens/SuperStock, pp. 42, 54; © Mjpix/Dreamstime.com, p. 43; © Ron Giling/Lineair/Photolibrary, p. 44; © Richard Wareham Fotografie/Alamy, pp. 46–47; © ED OUDENAARDEN/AFP/Getty Images, p. 48 (top); © akg-images, p. 48 (bottom); © INTERFOTO/Alamy, p. 50 (left); © Ulf Andersen/Getty Images, p. 50 (right); © VALERIE KUYPERS/AFP/Getty Images, p. 53; © DC Productions/Photodisc/Getty Images, pp. 56–57; © Lonely Planet/SuperStock, p. 58; © Frans Lemmens/Photographer's Choice/Getty Images, p. 59; © Devy/Dreamstime.com, p. 59 (inset); © Peter Horree/Alamy, p. 61; © iStockphoto.com/Clicks, p. 63; © [apply pictures]/Alamy, p. 64; © Ispace/Dreamstime.com, p. 68; © Laura Westlund/Independent Picture Service, p. 69.

Front cover: © Visions Of Our Land/Workbook Stock/Getty Images.
Back cover: NASA.